One Pot French

One Pot French

JEAN-PIERRE CHALLET

with

JENNIFER DECORTE

SELLERS
PUBLISHING

A SELLERS PUBLISHING/MADISON PRESS BOOK

Published by Sellers Publishing, Inc.
P.O. Box 818, Portland, Maine 04104
For ordering information:
(800) 625-3386 toll free
(207) 772-6814 fax

Visit our Web site: www.rsvp.com
E-mail: rsp@rsvp.com

President and Publisher: Ronnie Sellers
Publishing Director: Robin Haywood
Senior Editor: Megan Hiller

ISBN 13: 978-1-4162-0525-8

Library of Congress Control Number: 2008923440
10 9 8 7 6 5 4 3 2 1

Text, cover, design and compilation © 2008 The Madison Press Limited
Recipe text: © 2008 Jean-Pierre Challet
All photographs by Gareth Morgans except as noted on p 191

Produced by
Madison Press Books
1000 Yonge Street, Suite 200
Toronto, ON
M4W 2K2
madisonpressbooks.com

Printed in China by SNP Leefung, China

Contents

INTRODUCTION

MY STARTING POINT was to ask myself: "How does the concept of one pot apply to French cuisine?" Surely it seems like a contradiction. French cooking is about complexities. It is about being refined. Can this all happen in a single pot? I think it can. I admit I may bend the parameters in certain places, but the concept is about good food. Simple but good. Accessible but special. I approached this book with those thoughts in mind. Because I believe first and always in balance. Simple flavors have their value, but so do complexities. Traditions are vital, but so is exploration.

My hope is that these recipes make a good base for exploring. The Basic Recipes (see p. 9) form the foundation for all French cooking, and you might decide, after trying a few dishes, to prepare some sauces and stocks for your pantry, so they're on hand when you need to whip up a one-pot dish in a hurry. Or experiment by pairing dishes here and there, depending on your mood or the season. Though many of the featured soups, salads, and sandwiches are filling enough to eat on their own, don't be afraid to break the one-pot rule once in a while; when combined with other recipes, these singular dishes become simple, delicious full-course meals.

Cooking is about engaging all of your senses. The making and sharing of food should always be a wonderful experience. So as you cook, be aware of what it is about the food that most appeals to you. Is it the color? The texture? The aroma? Focus on that quality. Understand it. Then try to shape it toward your intended experience. That is the goal in cooking.

The notion of simplicity enters the world of French cuisine from the perspective of the end product. The goal is always to bring out the best in whatever it is you may be preparing. It is about clean, pure flavors preserved and heightened through ingredients and techniques.

Is French food always rich? Does it have to be difficult to make? I say no. Two of the most important ingredients in good cooking are time and attention to detail. Make good use of both and the food that comes out of your pot will always be a pleasure to you and those you serve.

JEAN-PIERRE CHALLET

Recettes de Base
Basic Recipes

BOUQUET GARNI
Bouquet garni

Used in stocks, soups, and slow-cooking dishes, a bouquet garni is a tied bundle of herbs, with a bay leaf and sprigs of thyme and parsley as the base. These are wrapped, often with other herbs and vegetables, in a piece of leek green or cheesecloth and tied together with string. Once its flavor has been extracted, the bouquet garni is removed from the dish. It is best to use fresh herbs, although dried can also be used.

1 bay leaf
few sprigs thyme
few sprigs parsley
black peppercorns
leek

FOND BLANC DE VOLAILLE
Chicken stock

Stock that is cooked too aggressively may become cloudy. Instead, simmer the stock slowly, frequently skimming off the fat and impurities that rise to the top.

Lemon pith can be bitter, so when preparing whole lemons to use in stocks (or in soups or poaching liquids), slice off the pith and use only the center part or the body of the lemon.

An onion clouté is a peeled, whole, halved, or quartered onion studded with a bay leaf and one or two cloves. It's an easy way to add flavor to stocks, stews, and sauces. Because the smaller elements are attached to large pieces of onion, they're easily retrieved. When they have released their flavor, their job is done.

Stock freezes very well. Portion into 2-cup/500 ml containers for easy use.

Note: Chicken carcasses can be purchased at most butcher shops, or ask the butcher at your local grocery-store meat counter. He or she will often sell you soup bones at minimal charge.

MAKES ABOUT 8 CUPS/2 LITERS

1 chicken, cut into pieces

2 chicken legs, cut into pieces

3 chicken carcasses, chopped

2 large sweet onions, peeled and halved

1 bay leaf

2 cloves

2 leeks, white part only, chopped

2 carrots, chopped

1 celery root, peeled and quartered

2-inch (5 cm) piece gingerroot, cut at both ends

1 lemon, pith removed, sliced

1 bouquet garni (see p. 10)

1 head of garlic, unpeeled, halved (optional)

Rinse the meat and bones. Place in a large heavy-bottomed pot and pour in enough cold water to cover the meat and bones completely. Bring to a boil, then immediately reduce heat to a simmer. Cook 20–30 minutes, skimming the stock frequently to remove any fat and impurities. To prevent the stock from getting cloudy, don't stir or move the bones too much while they're cooking.

Make an onion clouté with one of the onion halves by piercing the bay leaf and then the onion with the cloves.

Add the onion clouté, the remaining onion, leeks, carrot, celery root, gingerroot, lemon slices, bouquet garni, and garlic to the stock. Simmer for at least 3 hours.

Strain the stock into containers. Refrigerate as soon as it is cool, letting it sit until the fat rises to the top of the containers. If transferring to the freezer, remove the fat. If storing in the fridge, leave the fat — it's an ideal airtight seal that keeps the stock fresh for longer. Remove the fat before use.

FUMET DE POISSON
Fish stock

MAKES ABOUT 6 CUPS/1.5 LITERS

5 lbs/2.5 kg fish and fish bones, cut into pieces

1 large onion, peeled and halved

2 bay leaves

2 cloves

2 tbsp/30 ml unsalted butter

4 shallots, chopped

3 slices lemon, pith removed

1 bouquet garni (see p. 10)

½ bunch flat-leaf parsley

salt

Rinse the fish bones.

Make an onion clouté by piercing a bay leaf and then half an onion with a clove. Repeat with the second onion half.

Melt the butter in a large skillet or heavy-bottomed pot over low heat. Cook the shallots gently in the skillet, uncovered, until soft and translucent; do not allow to color. Add the fish pieces and bones, onion cloutés, lemon, bouquet garni, and parsley. Season with salt to taste. Pour in enough cold water to completely cover the fish. Simmer for 30 minutes, skimming off any impurities. Strain and let cool.

Freeze in 2-cup/500 ml batches for easy use for up to 6 months, or store in the refrigerator for 1 week.

CONFIT DE CANARD
Duck confit

Duck fat is widely available in specialty food shops and some butcher shops.
Note: Choose a fatty duck for this recipe. The duck needs to sit overnight in the seasonings, so plan ahead.

4 duck legs, skin on, thigh attached
  to drumstick

2 cloves garlic, germ removed,
  finely chopped

4 tbsp/60 ml chopped flat-leaf parsley

kosher salt

30 oz/850 g (approx. 4 cups/1 liter) duck fat

Rub the meat side (non-skin side) of the duck legs with the garlic and parsley. Sprinkle lightly with salt, cover, and refrigerate overnight.

Transfer the duck legs to a large heavy-bottomed pot or casserole dish, placing them side by side, skin-side down. Bring to room temperature.

In another pot, heat the duck fat to 195°F (90°C); do not leave the hot fat unattended. Gently pour the fat over the duck, covering it completely. Cook, covered, over low heat (or in a 275°F (135°C) oven) for 4 hours or until the duck is very tender.

Remove the duck to a resealable glass container and carefully strain the fat of any particles. Ladle enough warm duck fat over the duck meat to completely cover it, to form an airtight seal. Be sure to cover with fat and not the cooking juices. Keep refrigerated, removing the duck legs as needed, and resealing the confit each time by reheating the solidified fat. Or store the confit in smaller portions to avoid having to reseal it. Properly stored, duck confit will keep for up to 1 month.

PÂTE BRISÉE
Savory tart pastry

For best results, make the full recipe, storing any leftovers in the freezer, wrapped tightly in plastic wrap, for up to 6 months.

MAKES ABOUT 18 OZ/500 G (enough for two 9-inch (23 cm) tart shells or
   twenty 3 ½-inch (9 cm) tartlets)

1 ¾ cups/425 ml all-purpose flour	¼ tsp/1 ml salt
¾ cup plus 2 tbsp/200 ml cold, unsalted butter, cut into large dice	1 egg
	2 egg yolks

In a food processor, pulse flour, butter, and salt until just incorporated; the texture should be coarse. Add the egg, egg yolks, and 2 tbsp/30 ml of cold water; pulse until the dough gathers itself into a ball. Be careful not to overprocess. Add a few drops of cold water if the mixture is too dry.

Transfer the dough to a lightly floured surface and knead it for 1–2 minutes, until the dough is smooth and comes away easily from the work surface. Form the dough into a ball, flattening slightly. Cover with plastic wrap and refrigerate until firm, about 30 minutes.

On a lightly floured surface, roll out the dough, working quickly so that it doesn't get too soft to handle. Gently place the dough over a tart pan, pressing it into the bottom and sides. With your fingers, overlap the dough a little bit inside the rim. Trim off the excess. Gently pinch the dough up the sides of the pan to just slightly increase the height of the shell. If the dough is too soft to do this, chill it for a few minutes in the refrigerator. Blind bake, then fill and bake according to recipe.

Blind baking:
To bake a 9-inch (23 cm) tart, preheat the oven to 375°F (190°C). Prick the bottom of the tart shell in several places with a fork, to prevent the dough from bubbling. Line the tart shell with parchment paper and fill with pie weights or dried beans or rice. Bake for 5 minutes. Lower the heat to 350°F (180°C); remove the weights. Bake for another 5 minutes or until the pastry is a pale, very light brown. If baking 3 ½-inch (9 cm) tartlets, reduce the baking time from 5 minutes to 3 minutes for both steps.

PÂTE SABLÉE
Sweet tart pastry

For best results, make the full recipe, storing any leftovers in the freezer, wrapped tightly in plastic wrap, for up to 6 months.

MAKES ABOUT 18 OZ/500 G (enough for two 9-inch (23 cm) tart shells or twenty 3 ½-inch (9 cm) tartlets)

1 ¾ cups/425 ml all-purpose flour	pinch of salt
½ cup/125 ml sugar	¾ cup/175 ml cold unsalted butter, cubed
2 tbsp/30 ml vanilla sugar	1 egg

In a food processor, pulse together the flour, sugars, and salt. Add the butter and pulse until just incorporated and the mixture has a coarse texture.

Add the egg and then 1 tbsp/15 ml cold water; pulse until the dough gathers itself into a ball. Be careful not to overprocess. Add a few drops of cold water if the mixture is too dry.

Transfer the dough to a lightly floured surface and knead it for 1–2 minutes, until the dough is smooth and comes away easily from the work surface. The dough should be slightly crumbly. Form it into a ball, flattening slightly. Cover with plastic wrap and refrigerate until firm, about 30 minutes.

On a lightly floured surface, roll out the dough, working quickly so that it doesn't get too soft to handle. Gently place the dough over a tart pan, pressing it into the bottom and sides. With your fingers, overlap the dough a little bit inside the rim. Trim off the excess. Gently pinch the dough up the sides of the pan to just slightly increase the height of the shell. If the pastry is too soft to do this, chill it for a few minutes in the refrigerator. Blind bake (see p. 14), then fill and bake according to recipe.

PÂTE FEUILLETÉE
Puff pastry crust

Topping a soup with a crust of puff pastry adds a lot to its visual presentation.
Use this crust with chilled soup, as it will heat in the oven as the crust bakes.

SERVES 4

9 oz/250 g puff pastry   pinch of salt

1 egg

Preheat oven to 350°F (180°C).

Ladle chilled soup into ovenproof bowls, leaving at least 1 inch (2.5 cm) at the top.
Do not overfill.

Cut a sheet of puff pastry into a round about 2 inches (5 cm) wider than the diameter
of the soup bowl. Place the sheet on the top of the bowl, letting the sides fold over the
rim; pinch lightly to secure.

In a small bowl, combine the egg, a pinch of salt, and 2 tbsp/30 ml water. Brush the
pastry with the egg wash. Bake the soup with the pastry crust for 15–20 minutes or
until golden brown.

ROYALE
Royale mixture

This egg mixture is used in many egg tarts such as goat-cheese tarts and quiche.

Use this filling with blind baked (partially baked) tart shells (see p. 14), unless the tarts are very small.

MAKES ABOUT 1¾ CUPS/425 ML (enough for one 9-inch (23 cm)
tart or eight 4-inch (10 cm) tartlets)

2 eggs

2 egg yolks

½ cup/125 ml milk

½ cup/125 ml whipping cream

salt and pepper

Gently whisk together the eggs, egg yolks, milk, and cream. Season with salt and pepper. Place other ingredients your recipe calls for in the tart shell; top with royale mixture, to about two-thirds full, unless recipe specifies otherwise. Bake as directed.

CRÊPES
Crepes

The way your crepes turn out depends on both the consistency of the batter and the pan used. A crepe pan or small, shallow, nonstick skillet works best. Classic French crepe pans have changed very little since the seventeenth century. Traditionally made of steel, these pans need to be seasoned; nonstick pans are now also available. Crepe pans have an upward tilting handle, making it easy to swirl the batter, and are shallow with sloping sides, for easier flipping and removing of the crepes. Crepes can be made in a wide variety of sizes, from tiny to dinner-plate size. Don't worry about making perfect crepes the first time — you may need to make a few to get the hang of it. *Note: For sweet crepes, add 1 tbsp/15 ml of sugar to the flour.*

SERVES 4–6 (15–30 crepes, depending on the crepe size)

1 ½ cups/375 ml all-purpose flour	2 cups/500 ml whole milk
pinch of salt	¼ cup/50 ml unsalted butter, melted
4 eggs	nonstick cooking spray or butter, for cooking

Sift the flour into a bowl. Add the salt. Make a well in the center of the flour and break the eggs into it. Whisking in the center of the mixture, slowly draw the flour in until it is fully mixed. Gradually add the milk and then the butter, whisking to a smooth consistency. The batter should be runny enough to thinly coat the back of a spoon; add a little more milk if it is too stiff. Let batter sit for 30 minutes, wrapped, in the refrigerator.

Coat the pan lightly with a small amount of nonstick cooking spray or butter over medium heat. Test that the pan is hot enough by putting a drop of batter in it — it should spatter briskly. Add a ladle of batter to the pan. Use about ¼ cup/50 ml for a small crepe and about ⅓ cup/75 ml for a larger crepe. Tilt the pan so that the batter coats the bottom evenly. Cook until set, about 1 minute. Loosen the crepe with a spatula; flip over with the spatula or a flick of the wrist. Cook the second side for about another minute.

Stack crepes to keep them moist and warm.

POLENTA
Polenta

This is a recipe for a firm polenta.

Note: If you prefer not to use garlic, simply warm the milk, then add the butter.

MAKES ABOUT 1 ½ CUPS/375 ML

1 cup/250 ml milk

2 cloves garlic, peeled, whole

2 tbsp/30 ml unsalted butter

¼ cup/50 ml very fine cornmeal

1 egg

2 tbsp/30 ml shredded Tomme de Savoie cheese

salt and pepper

Lightly oil a shallow baking dish.

In a medium-sized saucepan over medium heat, heat the milk with the garlic to just under the boil; remove from heat and let steep for 2–3 minutes or until the desired amount of garlic flavor has been imparted to the milk.

Add the butter to the infused milk; bring to a boil, stirring to incorporate the butter. Remove the garlic and discard. Slowly pour in the cornmeal, stirring with a wooden spoon until the cornmeal is well incorporated. Stir in the egg; cook for 1 minute. Add the cheese, stirring until melted. Season with salt and pepper.

Pour the mixture into the baking dish; flatten with a spoon. Chill, uncovered, in the refrigerator for about 1 hour or until firm. Once set, cut into portions with a cookie cutter. Just before serving, sauté the polenta in hot oil until heated through and golden brown.

BEURRE COMPOSÉ AU CITRON
Composed lemon butter

MAKES ABOUT 1 CUP/250 ML

zest of 2 lemons

1 cup/250 ml unsalted butter, softened

juice of 4 lemons

salt and pepper to taste

1 sprig thyme, leaves picked and
   finely chopped

Blanch the lemon zest: in a small pot, bring a small amount of cold water and the lemon zest to a boil. As soon as it reaches the boil, strain. Repeat this process three times, to remove any bitterness from the lemon zest. Set the strained zest aside to cool.

In a food processor or mixer with a paddle attachment, mix the zest, butter, lemon juice, and salt and pepper until combined and slightly creamy. Mix in the thyme.

Tear a sheet of plastic wrap and put it on your work surface. With a spatula, place the butter on the plastic wrap. Roll it up into a log, twisting the ends of the plastic to seal. Chill or freeze, cutting off slices as needed.

MAYONNAISE
Mayonnaise

MAKES 4 CUPS/1 LITER

4 egg yolks

3 tbsp/45 ml Dijon mustard

3 cups/750 ml grapeseed oil

6 tbsp/90 ml freshly squeezed lemon juice

salt and pepper

Bring all ingredients to room temperature. In a food processor, blend the egg yolks and mustard until the mixture begins to thicken. Add about 3 tbsp/45 ml of the oil, a few drops at a time, continuing to blend in the food processor. Add the remaining oil in a very slow stream, blending constantly. The mayonnaise should be thick and glossy, and should just hold its shape. To finish, add the lemon juice, season with salt and pepper, and blend to incorporate.

Aïoli (Garlic mayonnaise)
Add 4 or 5 cloves of mashed cloves of garlic to eggs and mustard.

Mustard mayonnaise
Add an extra 2 tbsp/30 ml of Dijon mustard to the paste.

KETCHUP AUX TOMATES MAISON
Tomato ketchup

MAKES ABOUT 6 CUPS/1.5 LITERS

2 tbsp/30 ml grapeseed oil

2 lbs/1 kg red onion, sliced

2 lbs/1 kg tomatoes, chopped

1 cup/250 ml honey

1 cup/250 ml balsamic vinegar

1 tbsp/15 ml ground ginger

½ cup/125 ml brown sugar

1 cup/250 ml sherry vinegar

1 tbsp/15 ml cayenne pepper

1 tbsp/15 ml paprika

2 tbsp/30 ml Dijon mustard

salt to taste

In a large heavy-bottomed pot, heat the oil over low heat. Add the onion and lightly sweat until it is soft and translucent; do not allow to color. Add the remaining ingredients and gently simmer for about 2 hours. Blend and pass through a large-holed strainer. Refrigerated, the ketchup will keep for about 2 weeks.

TAPENADE
Olive tapenade

MAKE AS MUCH AS DESIRED, USING A RATIO OF 3 PARTS OLIVES
TO 1 PART DRESSING

pitted, oil-packed black olives (dried Moroccan or your favorite variety)
lemon vinaigrette (see p. 27)

Process the olives in a food processor until well chopped. Add the lemon vinaigrette; process to incorporate to a paste. Refrigerate in a sealed glass jar for up to 1 month.

SAUCE BÉCHAMEL
Béchamel sauce

MAKES ABOUT 4 CUPS/1 LITER

½ Spanish or other sweet onion,
   peeled and halved

1 bay leaf

1 whole clove

2 cups/500 ml whole milk

2 cups/500 ml whipping cream

2 tbsp/30 ml unsalted butter

3 tbsp/45 ml all-purpose flour

salt and white pepper

Make an onion clouté by piercing the bay leaf and then one onion half with the clove. Chop the other onion half. Put all the onion into a large bowl.

Heat the milk and cream in a heavy-bottomed saucepan to just under the boil. Pour the hot milk mixture over the onions. Let stand for about 10 minutes for the flavors to infuse and for the milk to cool. Strain the milk mixture, discarding the solids.

In the same saucepan, melt the butter over medium heat. Whisk in the flour and cook for about 2 minutes, stirring constantly. The roux should be bubbling but not browned. Gradually add the milk mixture, whisking constantly to prevent lumps. Continue to stir until the sauce is smooth and creamy. Reduce the heat; simmer the sauce for 5–10 minutes or until it thickens enough to coat the back of a spoon. Remove from heat. Season with salt and white pepper.

SAUCE ROUILLE
Rouille sauce

If you can't find piquillo peppers, substitute red bell peppers, to give the sauce its rich red-orange color. You can roast your own red peppers: put them directly on the burner if you have a gas stove, or place them on a baking sheet and roast in a 400°F (200°C) oven. When completely blackened, put the peppers into a bowl and cover with plastic wrap; set aside for at least 10 minutes. The steam will cause the blackened skin to separate from the flesh, making the peppers easy to peel. Remove all the char from the outside of the pepper. Cut the peppers into pieces, discarding the stem and seeds. You'll also find roasted red peppers at your local deli counter.

MAKES ABOUT 4 CUPS/1 LITER

juice of 2 lemons

pinch of saffron

¼ cup/50 ml chopped garlic (or to taste)

3 egg yolks

3–5 piquillo peppers (or 1–2 red peppers)

1–2 tbsp/15–30 ml Dijon mustard

2 cups/500 ml olive oil

1 cup/250 ml grapeseed oil

salt and white pepper

In a small pot over low heat, heat the lemon juice with the saffron. Remove from heat; cool to room temperature.

In a food processor, combine the garlic, egg yolks, peppers, and mustard. Pulse to mix, then purée until smooth. Add about 3 tbsp/45 ml of the olive oil, a few drops at a time, mixing constantly. Add the remaining olive oil and the grapeseed oil in a slow stream, continuing to mix. The rouille should be thick, glossy, and just hold its shape, similar to mayonnaise.

To finish, add the saffron-infused lemon juice and season with salt and white pepper, blending to incorporate. Store, covered, in the refrigerator for up to 1 week.

SAUCE RAVIGOTE
Ravigot dressing

Ravigot dressing is basically an herb mayonnaise. The herbs should be finely chopped; the dressing will have a slight greenish tint.

MAKES 2 CUPS/500 ML

1 egg yolk, at room temperature

2 hard-cooked egg yolks,
   at room temperature

1 tbsp/15 ml mayonnaise (see p. 21)
   or use store-bought

1 tbsp/15 ml Dijon mustard

1 tsp/5 ml each tarragon,
   chervil, and parsley

½ cup/125 ml grapeseed oil

4 tsp/20 ml freshly squeezed lemon juice

salt and pepper

In a food processor, blend the egg yolks, mayonnaise, mustard, and herbs, slowly adding about 1 tbsp/15 ml of the oil, a few drops at a time. Add the remaining oil in a steady stream. Add the lemon juice, and the salt and pepper to taste; blend until the herbs are finely chopped. Store, covered, in the refrigerator for up to 1 week.

SAUCE MALTAISE
Maltaise sauce

Maltaise sauce is simply Hollandaise sauce with blood orange juice.

MAKES ABOUT I CUP/250 ML

4 egg yolks	juice of ½ lemon
¾ cup/175 ml unsalted butter, softened	juice of 1 blood orange
4 tbsp/60 ml dry white wine	salt and pepper

Bring all ingredients to room temperature. In a large metal bowl, whisk the egg yolks. Set the bowl over a pan of simmering water and continue whisking, maintaining a gentle heat and using an even motion to avoid scrambling the eggs. Whisk until the mixture makes a wide ribbon trail when the whisk is lifted from the bowl — at least 5 minutes.

Continue to whisk while adding a very small amount of the butter, then the rest bit by bit. The sauce's consistency should be thin enough to pour but thick enough to lightly coat a wooden spoon. Stir in the white wine, lemon juice, and blood orange juice. Season with salt and pepper.

VINAIGRETTE AU CITRON

Lemon vinaigrette

MAKES 2 CUPS/500 ML

6 tbsp/90 ml freshly squeezed lemon juice

3 tbsp/45 ml Dijon mustard

1 ¼ cups/300 ml grapeseed oil

salt and pepper

In a mini food processor or whisking by hand, blend together the lemon juice and mustard. Slowly add about 3 tbsp/45 ml of the oil, a few drops at a time. Add the remaining oil in a steady stream. Season with salt and pepper.

Keep refrigerated for up to 1 week.

VINAIGRETTE AU YAOURT

Yogurt dressing

MAKES 1 ½ CUPS/375 ML

1 tbsp/15 ml Dijon mustard

¼ cup/50 ml herb vinegar of your choice

⅔ cup/150 ml yogurt

½ cup/125 ml olive oil

¼ cup/50 ml grapeseed oil

salt and pepper

In a small food processor, blend together the mustard, vinegar, and yogurt. Slowly add about 2 tbsp/30 ml of the olive oil, a few drops at a time. Add the remaining olive oil and the grapeseed oil in a steady stream, continuing to blend. Season with salt and pepper.

Keep refrigerated for up to 1 week.

VINAIGRETTE À LA MOUTARDE
Mustard dressing

MAKES ABOUT ½ CUP/125 ML

2 tbsp/30 ml lemon juice

6 tbsp/90 ml grapeseed oil

1 tsp/5 ml Dijon mustard

1 tbsp/15 ml finely chopped shallots

salt and pepper to taste

In a small bowl, combine all ingredients. Store, covered, in the refrigerator for up to 1 week.

PISTOU DE POUSSES DE BASILIC VERT
Baby green basil pesto

This recipe makes a paste that is an excellent accompaniment to any fish, and can be spread on the serving plate or on the fish using a pastry brush. Corsica cheese is available at most specialty cheese shops.

MAKES ABOUT 1 CUP/250 ML

1 bunch baby green basil
   (approx. 40 leaves)

4 cloves garlic, germ removed

6 tbsp/90 ml pine nuts, lightly toasted

⅔ cup/150 ml olive oil

2 tbsp/30 ml Corsica cheese, finely grated

Put all ingredients into a mini-chopper or small food processor and mix until well blended. Store in a sealed jar in the refrigerator for up to 1 month.

CROÛTONS

Croutons

SERVES 4

1 crusty white baguette

2 tbsp/30 ml olive oil

1 clove garlic, halved (optional)

3 ½ oz/100 g Gruyère cheese, finely shredded (optional)

Preheat oven to 375°F (190°C).

Slice the baguette into thin rounds or cut thinly on the diagonal. Place the bread slices on a baking sheet; brush with the olive oil. Crisp in oven until a pale, golden brown. Remove from the oven and immediately rub the warm croutons with a cut side of the garlic, if using. Sprinkle the Gruyère cheese, if using, over top.

Les Entrées
Appetizers

Brandade de morue aux rattes /
Salt cod and fingerling potato dip   32

Calamars à la Sétoise / *Calamari with tomato and olives*   34

Galette de crabe et sar rouille /
Crab cakes with rouille sauce   36

Huitres à la vodka de bleuets sauvages /
Oysters with wild blueberry, lemon, and vodka   38

Jambon de Bayonne, trois melons, et figues /
Bayonne ham with melon and figs   39

Champignons farcis au chèvre d'herbes /
Portobello mushrooms stuffed with goat cheese and herbs   40

Roulade d'endive et saumon fumé aux deux caviars /
Smoked salmon in Belgian endive roulade with caviars   42

Steak tartare / *Steak tartare*   43

BRANDADE DE MORUE AUX RATTES

Salt cod and fingerling potato dip

In France, dried cod and fresh cod are treated as very different foods — they do not even share the same name. This recipe is an excellent example of how a rustic, simple, and common dish can be elevated to a delicacy with just a small touch. As is the custom in the south of France, garlic can be added to the brandade. To achieve a sweet, subtle garlic flavor, infuse the cream with three whole cloves of garlic.

Traditionally, the brandade is served as a warm dip with fingers of toast.

Note: Presoak the cod in water, refrigerated, for at least 3 days, changing the water several times to remove the salt.

SERVES 4

1 large onion, peeled

1 bay leaf

1 clove

1 ⅓ lbs/600 g boneless dry salt cod, soaked

2 cloves garlic

¾ cup/125 ml plus 2 tbsp/200 ml whipping cream

1 ⅓ cups/325 ml olive oil

2 fingerling potatoes, cooked and peeled

juice of 1 lemon

pinch of ground nutmeg

ground white pepper

½ recipe plain croutons (see p. 29)

Preheat oven to 350°F (180°C). Make an onion clouté by piercing the bay leaf and then the onion with the clove. Place the salt cod, onion clouté, and garlic cloves in a pot; cover with cold water. Bring to a simmer and cook for 10–15 minutes or until the cod is tender. Drain the cod and taste it. If the cod is still salty, return it to the pot, add fresh cold water, and bring it to a simmer, for about 5 minutes. Transfer the cod to a bowl and break into pieces.

Heat the cream in a small pot; do not allow to boil. Heat the olive oil in another pot.

Put the salt cod and fingerling potatoes in the bowl of a food processor. Process, gradually adding the warm oil, then the warm cream, through the feed tube. Add the lemon juice and nutmeg; season with white pepper. Serve warm with croutons.

CALAMARS À LA SÉTOISE

Calamari with tomato and olives

I prefer deep-frying squid to grilling it. The flavors are sealed in, the presentation is wonderful, and satisfaction is close to guaranteed. The soaking is a vital step for tenderness. This dish is named after Sete, a city in the south of France.

Note: The squid needs to be soaked, so plan ahead. Purchase the squid cleaned and ready to soak.

SERVES 4

8 whole squid (3–5-inch/8–12 cm body tubes)

2 cups/500 ml whole milk

½ lb/250 g fingerling potatoes, scrubbed

1 lb/500 g vine-ripened tomatoes

2 lemons

8 cups/2 liters vegetable oil, for frying

6 tbsp/90 ml good-quality extra virgin olive oil

2 cloves garlic, germ removed, chopped

⅔ cup/150 ml Niçoise olives

1 cup/250 ml grape tomatoes, halved

salt and pepper

all-purpose flour, for dredging

1 tbsp/15 ml finely chopped chives

1 tbsp/15 ml finely chopped flat-leaf parsley

Soak the squid in the milk overnight or for a few hours to tenderize it. Drain and discard the milk; pat the squid dry.

In a large pot, bring the potatoes to a boil in cold salted water; cook until tender. Drain and let cool.

Blanch the tomatoes in boiling water just long enough for the skin to separate from the flesh; refresh in cold water. Remove the skin and cut out the seeds, discarding both. Chop the flesh into chunks.

Zest the lemons, then peel and segment them.

In a deep-fryer or large pot, heat the vegetable oil to 335°F (170°C).

In the meantime, peel the potatoes, then slice into coins. Heat the olive oil in a large saucepan over medium heat. Add the garlic and chopped tomato; sauté for 2 minutes. Add the potato slices, olives, grape tomatoes, lemon zest and segments, plus ½ cup/125 ml of cold water. Gently cook for 2–3 minutes. Season with salt and pepper.

On a plate, lightly dredge the squid in flour, shaking off any excess. Deep-fry in the heated vegetable oil until light golden-brown, about 2 minutes. Drain on paper towel.

Serve at once in a warm bowl, accompanied by the tomato mixture and a sprinkling of chives and parsley.

GALETTE DE CRABE ET SAR ROUILLE

Crab cakes with rouille sauce

People tell me my crab cakes are lighter than expected. These cakes have no starches or bread in the mixture to weigh them down; only the outside is coated in breadcrumbs. I like to use panko, Japanese breadcrumbs, which are coarser than regular breadcrumbs. To me, an appetizer should be a tantalizing preview to the dinner.

Note: Although you can use store-bought mayonnaise in this recipe, it will affect the delicate flavor of this dish as some store-bought mayonnaise is sweet, some salty. It's definitely worth going the extra half-mile and making the mayonnaise from scratch.

SERVES 4

12 oz/360 g lump crab meat

2 sprigs cilantro

3 tbsp/45 ml mayonnaise (see p. 21) or use store-bought, adding more as needed

2 tbsp/30 ml chopped pickled ginger

salt and black pepper

⅓ cup/75 ml panko or regular breadcrumbs

vegetable oil, for frying

Gently squeeze out any excess moisture from the crab. Place the crab in a food processor with the cilantro, mayonnaise, pickled ginger, salt, and a pinch of pepper. Be generous when adding the mayonnaise — the mixture should be moist.

Process with a few short pulses to mix. Don't overprocess — the crab should still be somewhat chunky.

Use a 3-inch (8 cm) ring mold to uniformly form the crab mixture into four cakes. (Or use a smaller mold to make 8 small cakes.) The cakes should not be too thick or packed too tightly.

In a bowl, slightly crush the panko. Bread all sides of each crab cake with the panko. Refrigerate until needed.

To cook, heat a drop or two of the oil in a nonstick or heavy-bottomed skillet over medium heat. Cook the crab cakes until a light golden crust forms and crab is warmed through, about 1 minute per side.

These crab cakes go well with Rouille Sauce (see p. 24), a colorful, strongly flavored accompaniment that can be appreciated in small amounts. Use a pastry brush to spread a wide band on the serving plate, place the warm crab cakes on the sauce, and top with a mini salad or sautéed shrimp.

HUITRES À LA VODKA
DE BLEUETS SAUVAGES

Oysters with wild blueberry, lemon, and vodka

While the sweetness of the blueberries goes perfectly with oysters, there is also a textural relationship. I often hear them being compared to caviar: they have the same texture, and a cracking pop to the bite.

SERVES 4

2 tbsp/30 ml sugar

zest of 1 lemon

12 small cold-water oysters

2 tbsp/30 ml good-quality vodka

¼ cup/50 ml wild blueberries

In a small, heavy-bottomed saucepan, bring the sugar and 2 tbsp/30 ml of water to a boil. Reduce the liquid to a syrup-like consistency. Sir in half of the lemon zest; reserve the rest for garnish. Remove the pan from the heat and let the mixture cool.

Scrub the oysters under cold running water to clean. Open each oyster by holding it in a cloth in the palm of your hand. Insert the tip of an oyster knife at the shell hinge and carefully twist the knife to pop the shell open. Slide the knife along the inside of the top shell to sever the adductor muscle. Place the detached shell upside down on an individual serving plate or a serving platter. Drain the liquid from the oyster and with the knife tip loosen the oyster from the bottom shell. Position the bottom shell on an inverted top shell.

Top the oysters with vodka, blueberries, a dash of the lemon syrup, and a sprinkle of lemon zest. Serve at once.

JAMBON DE BAYONNE,
TROIS MELONS, ET FIGUES

Bayonne ham with melons and figs

The trick in this dish is to include a variety of flavors and textures, and to plate well. Each of the three melons used in this recipe has its own flavor and if they're about the same size, the arrangement on the plate is especially striking. The figs add further visual appeal — because the best meals always start with a "wow!"

Bayonnne is a French cured ham made in the southwest of France. The saltiness of the ham plays well with the sweet taste of melon. You'll find it at delicatessens, specialty food shops, and butcher shops.

SERVES 4

1 tbsp/15 ml finely chopped shallots	1 cantaloupe
1 tsp/5 ml Dijon mustard	1 honeydew melon
6 tbsp/90 ml extra virgin olive oil	1 canary melon
2 tbsp/30 ml Banyuls or balsamic vinegar	4 figs, ripe and firm, sliced into discs
1 tsp/5 ml lightly chopped chervil	8 slices Bayonne ham
1 tsp/5 ml finely chopped chives	

In a small metal bowl, whisk together the shallots, mustard, olive oil, vinegar, chervil, and chives.

Cut the cantaloupe, honeydew melon, and canary melon in half lengthwise; cut off and discard the two ends. Peel, seed, and thinly slice the melons.

To serve, arrange the melon slices attractively on a plate in a fan shape of alternating colors. Arrange the fig and ham slices attractively on the plate with the melon slices. Drizzle the dressing over top.

CHAMPIGNONS FARCIS
AU CHÈVRE D'HERBES

Portobello mushrooms stuffed with goat cheese and herbs

I like to think of this stuffed mushroom as a breadless sandwich. The flavors are undeniably and appealingly well matched, but your guests will likely comment as much on the tactile experience. This is an excellent dish during winter, when fresh produce is less readily available.

SERVES 4

8 portobello mushrooms,
    approx. 3 inches (8 cm) in diameter

3 tbsp/45 ml extra virgin olive oil

salt and pepper

2 shallots, finely chopped

2 tbsp/30 ml unsalted butter

½ lb/250 g chèvre, softened

1 tbsp/15 ml finely chopped chives

1 tbsp/15 ml finely chopped parsley

Stem the mushrooms, discarding the stems. Using a teaspoon, remove the gills and discard. Wipe off any dirt on the mushroom caps with paper towel.

In a sauté pan over medium heat, sauté the mushrooms caps in 1 tbsp/15 ml of the olive oil, season with salt and pepper. Remove from heat and let cool.

In an uncovered skillet over low heat, cook the shallots gently in the butter until tender and translucent.

Crumble the goat cheese into a small bowl. Mix in the warm shallots, chives, and parsley. Add the remaining 2 tbsp/30 ml olive oil a little at a time, stirring, until the mixture is slightly creamy.

When the mushrooms are cool, sparingly fill half the caps with the mixture. Don't overfill or the cheese may run out when heated. Put another cap on top of each to make a "sandwich." Refrigerate until needed.

To serve, heat mushrooms on a parchment-lined baking sheet in a 325°F (160°C) oven until hot, about 3–5 minutes. Serve at once.

ROULADE D'ENDIVE ET SAUMON
FUMÉ AUX DEUX CAVIARS

Smoked salmon in Belgian endive roulade with caviars

In this dish, the bitterness of the endive is offset by the sweetness of the salmon, and the overall effect is both unusual and distinctive.

SERVES 4

3 large endives

2 cups/500 ml whole milk

2 tbsp/30 ml mayonnaise (see p. 21)
    or use store-bought

1 tbsp/15 ml finely chopped pickled ginger

1 tbsp/15 ml lightly chopped chervil

7 oz/200 g smoked salmon

1 tbsp/15 ml large salmon roe

1 tbsp/15 ml sturgeon caviar, for garnish

Discard any torn or discolored leaves from the outside of the endives. With a sharp knife, gently score the bottom of each close to the root and carefully remove the leaves, discarding the smaller leaves and core. You should have enough leaves to reconstruct 2 endives. Pour the milk into a deep bowl. Submerse the endive leaves in the milk and soak for 1 hour or overnight.

To make the dressing, in a small bowl, mix the mayonnaise, pickled ginger, and half of the chervil. Set aside.

Remove the endives from the milk and pat dry with paper towel. Place a piece of salmon on one of the larger leaves. Place another leaf on top; fold over the sides of the salmon. Continue to layer the endive and salmon, gradually reassembling the endive with half of the leaves and half of the salmon.

Holding the reassembled endive firmly in one hand, lay it on a piece of plastic wrap. Pull the wrap around it, tightly twisting both ends to seal. Repeat with the remaining endive leaves and salmon. Refrigerate for at least 1 hour before serving. To serve, unwrap the endives, cut off the ends, and discard, then slice each endive crosswise into about 4 slices. Place 2 slices each into a Chinese spoon. Add a tiny dollop of the mayonnaise dressing and a sprinkling of roe and caviar. Top with the remaining chervil.

STEAK TARTARE

Steak tartare

The flavors and texture of the meat and dressing work wonderfully together in this dish, and the sense of freshness is undeniable. I substitute the traditional capers with gherkins as a matter of personal taste and a dedication to balance — I find that capers call a little too much attention to themselves. Finally, the Cognac has the complexity to intensify the meat's flavors beautifully.

SERVES 4

1 egg yolk

2 tbsp/30 ml finely chopped shallots

2 tbsp/30 ml Dijon mustard
   dash of Tabasco

splash of Worcestershire sauce

2 tbsp/30 ml grapeseed oil

1 tbsp/15 ml Cognac

salt and pepper

1 tbsp/15 ml finely chopped parsley

1 lb/500 g beef tenderloin

2 tbsp/30 ml finely chopped gherkin pickles

20 thin slices baguette, toasted or grilled

To make the dressing, in a food processor or large metal bowl, mix the egg yolk, shallots, and mustard. Mix in the Tabasco and Worcestershire sauces. Slowly add the oil, then the Cognac, continuing to mix. Season with a pinch of salt, pepper, and a pinch of the parsley.

Clean the meat of any silver skin, veins, or excess fat. Cut into thin strips with the grain. Chop the meat finely across the grain into very small pieces, ⅛ inch (3 mm) or smaller. Put the meat into a bowl and toss lightly with the shallot mixture to coat. Stir in the gherkins, salt and pepper to taste, and the remaining parsley.

Divide the meat evenly among four chilled plates, shaping into quenelles with two spoons or using a ring mold to shape. Arrange toasts on the plate beside the tartare. Serve at once.

Soupes
Soups

Soupe de poissons aux croûtons et rouille /
Fish soup with rouille croutons   46

Poisson à la plancha /
Seared fish bouillabaisse   48

Bisque de homard, crevettes, et gingembre /
Lobster bisque with shrimp and ginger   51

Bourride de loup de mer/
European bass fish stew   53

Soupe de carottes nouvelles et Fourme d'Ambert
aux noix de pacanes / *Carrot soup with toasted   54
pecans and Fourme d'Ambert cheese*

Crème de champignons et chanterelles /
Cream of button mushroom soup with chanterelles   57

Crème de maïs / *Corn soup*   58

Potage St Germain et pommes de terre confites /
Creamy sweet pea soup with fingerling potato confit   60

Vichyssoise / *Potato and leek soup*   62

Soupe de tomates petit déjeuner /
Breakfast tomato soup   65

Soupe à l'oignon gratinée / *French onion soup*   66

SOUPE DE POISSONS
AUX CROÛTONS ET ROUILLE

Fish soup with rouille croutons

This is the only spicy food that I am able to eat on a hot day. The flavors are so well balanced that the experience is always pleasant. Apart from anything else, the brilliant orange hue of this distinctive soup makes it a wonder on your table. As with all soups in this section, a Puff Pastry Crust (see p. 16) provides a lovely visual touch.

SERVES 4

4 whole whitings, cleaned but not scaled (approx. 5 lbs/2.5 kg in total)

2 tbsp/30 ml olive oil

1 medium onion, sliced

6 medium shallots, sliced

4 cloves garlic, crushed

¼ large fennel bulb, sliced

⅓ cup/75 ml sliced leek, white part only

2 stalks celery, chopped

1 bay leaf

1 large tomato, peeled, seeded, and chopped

5 sprigs parsley

4 sprigs thyme

salt and pepper

juice and zest of ¼ orange

½ tsp/2 ml saffron

4 baguette slices

3 ½ oz/100 g French Emmental cheese, finely grated

rouille sauce (see p. 24)

Cut the fish into large chunks or steaks, reserving the heads and tails. Heat the olive oil in a heavy-bottomed pot over medium heat. Add the fish, including the heads and tails; sauté lightly for 2 minutes.

Add the onion, shallots, and garlic; sauté for 1 minute. Add the fennel, leeks, celery, and bay leaf. In an uncovered pot, cook the vegetables gently until they are tender; do not allow them to color. Stir in the tomatoes. Add the parsley and thyme. Season with salt and pepper.

Add the orange juice and zest, saffron, and enough boiling water to completely cover. Bring to a gentle simmer for 15–20 minutes or until the fish pieces are falling apart. Purée and strain well.

To make the garnish, toast the baguette slices, brush with the rouille sauce using a pastry brush, and finish with a sprinkle of French Emmental cheese.

Gently ladle soup into warmed soup bowls. Float one crouton in each or serve on the side.

POISSON À LA PLANCHA

Seared fish bouillabaisse

The best possible way to enjoy this Mediterranean dish is to allow yourself to get messy. Traditionally served in a cork tray from the center of the table, this flavorful mélange is all about getting chunks of what captures your fancy and talking with your mouth full.

You can serve it with Croutons (see p. 29) and shredded Gruyère cheese, with Rouille Sauce (see p. 24) or Dijon mustard on the side.

Note: Ask your fishmonger to clean, scale, and fillet the fish. Be sure the pin bones are removed. Wrap well in plastic wrap and refrigerate until needed. Ask your fishmonger for fish bones for this recipe, too.

SERVES 4

3 shallots	1 lb/500 g fish bones
½ medium onion	3 cloves garlic, germ removed
½ small celery root	8 sprigs parsley
¼ fennel bulb	2 sprigs thyme
⅓ cup/75 ml sliced leek, white part only	1 bay leaf
1 orange	pinch of saffron
1 1–2-lb/500 g whole red snapper, filleted	2 tbsp/30 ml tomato paste
	2 Yukon Gold potatoes
1 2-lb/1 kg whole striped bass, filleted	salt and pepper

To prepare the *mirepoix*, the mixture of vegetables to be used as a flavoring, roughly dice the shallots, onion, celery root, fennel, and leeks.

Use a vegetable peeler to remove strips of peel from the orange, leaving behind as much of the white pith as possible.

Cut each fish fillet in half. Heat about two-thirds of the olive oil in a large heavy-bottomed pot over medium heat. When the oil is hot, add the fish bones. Sweat the fish bones for a few minutes, without allowing them to color. Add the *mirepoix*, garlic, orange peel, parsley, thyme, bay leaf, and saffron; sweat the mixture for a few minutes.

Stir in the tomato paste. Add water to just barely cover the bones. Over medium heat, bring the bouillabaisse to a gentle simmer, cover, and cook for 30 minutes. Season with salt and pepper.

In the meantime, peel and cut the potatoes into 1-inch (2.5 cm) cubes. Place the potatoes in a large pot of cold salted water and bring to a simmer; cook until tender. Drain and reserve.

Heat the remaining olive oil in a large sauté pan over medium-high heat. Sear the fish fillets until golden brown.

Add the potatoes to the bouillabaisse and heat through. Adjust seasoning as needed. Ladle servings into hot, shallow bowls and garnish with the fish.

BISQUE DE HOMARD, CREVETTES,
ET GINGEMBRE

Lobster bisque with shrimp and ginger

Any time you prepare lobster at home, make sure you save the shells; there is so much flavor in them that it is always worth using them to prepare a bisque. In this case, the bisque is enriched by the blend of cooked alcohols.

SERVES 4

For lobster stock:

1 leek, white part only, chopped

1 tbsp/15 ml olive oil

1 head garlic, unpeeled, halved

6 cups/1.5 liters fish stock (see p. 12)
    or store-bought

3 vine-ripened tomatoes

4 sprigs tarragon

1-inch/2.5 cm piece gingerroot, peeled

For bisque:

2 1½-lb/750 g lobsters (frozen or fresh)

⅓ cup/75 ml olive oil

1 carrot, chopped

1 onion, chopped

4 vine-ripened tomatoes, chopped

1 tbsp/15 ml tomato paste

2 cups/500 ml dry white wine

½ cup/125 ml Cognac

½ fennel bulb, chopped

1 bouquet garni (see p. 10)

4 sprigs tarragon

1 sprig flat-leaf parsley

1 head garlic, unpeeled, halved

1-inch (2.5 cm) piece gingerroot, peeled

2 slices soft white bread, crust removed, cubed

2 tbsp/30 ml Pernod

¼ cup/50 ml crème fraîche

salt and pepper

¼ cup/50 ml unsalted butter (optional)

4 cooked shrimp, peeled

gingerroot, for garnish

To make the lobster stock, sweat the leek in the olive oil for 1 minute. Add garlic; cook 1 minute. Add the fish stock, tomatoes, tarragon, and gingerroot; simmer gently for 5 minutes.

With the heel of a sharp knife or cleaver, chop both lobsters into 2-inch/5 cm pieces. In a Dutch oven or cocotte, sauté the lobster pieces (including shells) in 2 tbsp/30 ml heated olive oil for about 2 minutes. Add the carrot, onion, tomatoes, and tomato paste; sauté for 2 minutes. Pour in the lobster stock.

Pour the white wine and Cognac into a small heavy-bottomed pot; ignite with a match to remove the alcohol. Once the flame has died down, pour the liquid into the lobster mixture. Stir in the fennel, bouquet garni, tarragon, parsley, garlic, and gingerroot. Simmer for 30 minutes.

Remove the bouquet garni. Process the mixture in a heavy-duty blender (including shells); strain back into the pot. Stir in the bread, Pernod, and crème fraîche; simmer for 15 minutes. Blend and strain. Season with salt and pepper. To finish, blend in the butter, if using, just before serving.

To serve, place 1 shrimp at the bottom of each bowl, topped with a scant amount of freshly grated or extremely finely chopped gingerroot. Ladle soup on top and serve immediately.

BOURRIDE DE LOUP DE MER

European bass fish stew

People who say that mayonnaise cannot be served hot are wrong. This mayonnaise-based soup is delicious and thick enough to serve as a sauce.

SERVES 4

2 1–1½-lb/500–750 g European bass, filleted, heads, tails, and skin reserved

1 carrot, roughly diced

1 onion, roughly diced

1 leek, trimmed and halved

2 cloves garlic

1 slice orange

2 cups/500 ml fish stock (see p. 12) or use store-bought

2 cups/500 ml dry white wine

2 baby carrots, cleaned and cut lengthwise, green tops on

¼ medium celery root, diced

1 shallot, diced

pinch of saffron

½ cup/125 ml garlic mayonnaise (see p. 21)

juice of 1 lemon

To prepare the poaching liquid (*court bouillon*), place the fish heads, tails, skin, and bones in a large pot, along with the carrot, onion, leek, garlic, orange slice, fish stock, and white wine. Heat to a simmer; cook very gently for 30 minutes. Strain the liquid, discarding the solids. Return the liquid to the pot. Add the baby carrots, celery root, shallot, and saffron; cook for about 5 minutes or until vegetables are just tender.

Strain, reserving the liquid and setting the vegetables aside, covered with foil to keep warm. Return the liquid to the pot; bring it back to a gentle simmer. Add the bass fillets and poach for 2 minutes. Remove the fish with a wide-slotted spoon and set aside with the vegetables.

Strain any fish bits from the broth and return it to a simmer. To finish, whisk in the garlic mayonnaise and lemon juice.

Serve at once. Place a layer of vegetables, topped with one bass fillet, in a warmed rimmed soup bowl. Cover with the broth. If you like, accompany with croutons (see p. 29) and a quenelle of salt cod brandade (see p. 32).

SOUPE DE CAROTTES NOUVELLES
ET FOURME D'AMBERT AUX NOIX DE PACANES

Carrot soup with toasted pecans and Fourme d'Ambert cheese

This is an excellent dish that balances the sweetness of the carrots with the nuttiness of the pecan and perfectly sets the stage for the blue cheese accent. Fourme d'Ambert cheese is from the volcanic region of Auvergne, in central France.

SERVES 4

2 lbs/1 kg young carrots, peeled

1 medium onion, chopped

¼ cup/50 ml unsalted butter

2 fingerling potatoes, peeled and diced

4 cups/1 liter water or chicken stock (see p. 10)

1 sprig thyme

1 leek, white and light green part only, chopped

2 tbsp/30 ml whipping cream

salt and pepper

For garnish:

½ cup/125 ml pecan halves

2 tbsp/30 ml maple syrup

3 oz/80 g Fourme d'Ambert cheese

1 tbsp/15 ml chopped chives

Slice 4 of the carrots in half lengthwise; dice the rest.

In an uncovered skillet over low heat, cook the onions gently in half of the butter until soft and translucent; do not allow them to color. Add the diced carrots and sauté 2–3 minutes. Add the potato, water or stock, and thyme. Simmer for 10 minutes.

Poach the 8 carrot halves in the broth for 2–3 minutes — they should be firm but not overcooked. Remove the carrot halves and set aside, covered, to keep warm.

Preheat oven to 400°F (200°C).

Add the leeks to the broth; simmer for 5 minutes. Remove the thyme sprig from the broth. Purée the broth with a hand blender or in a blender. Add the remaining butter and the cream. Season with salt and pepper.

In the meantime, prepare pecans for the garnish. Toss the pecans in the maple syrup and transfer to a parchment paper-lined baking sheet. Bake in a 400°F (200°C) oven for about 5 minutes or until shiny and fragrant.

Ladle the soup into warmed rimmed soup bowls. In the center of each, criss-cross 2 sliced carrots to form an X, or simply float on top. Crumble the Fourme d'Ambert cheese where the carrots intersect; top with the warm pecans. Serve at once.

CRÈME DE CHAMPIGNONS
ET CHANTERELLES

Cream of button mushroom soup with chanterelles

Here, the cheapest, most common, and least considered mushroom finally gets its due. The darker, nuttier, or more musky varieties would overpower the intent of this recipe, which calls for a subtle touch.

SERVES 4

3 ½ oz/100 g chanterelle mushrooms, thickly sliced

2 tbsp/30 ml unsalted butter, plus 1 tbsp/15 ml (optional)

2 shallots, sliced

1 fingerling potato, peeled, cut into small dice

7 oz/200 g button mushrooms, sliced

1 bouquet garni (see p. 10)

salt and pepper

1 leek, white part only, sliced

½ cup/125 ml whipping cream

finely chopped chives, for garnish

In a skillet, sauté the chanterelles in 1 tbsp/15 ml butter until tender. Remove from heat, reserving as a garnish for the soup.

In a heavy-bottomed saucepan, sauté the shallots in 1 tbsp/15 ml butter. Add the potatoes and button mushrooms; sauté for 1 minute. Add about 2 cups/500 ml water, or enough to cover, and the bouquet garni. Season with salt and pepper. Simmer gently for 10 minutes. Stir in the leek and half of the cream. Simmer for another 5 minutes. Remove the bouquet garni.

Blend the soup until very smooth in a blender or with a hand blender. Add the rest of the cream, and, if you like, blend in 1 tbsp/15 ml butter for extra richness and flavor.

Ladle the soup into warmed bowls, placing a few chanterelles in the center. Sprinkle with chives and serve.

CRÈME DE MAÏS

Corn soup

Where I come from in France, the farmers do not see corn as food for people. That always struck me as crazy, so I developed this recipe to fly in the face of convention. It is extremely versatile and can be served with a variety of garnishes, such as sliced tomatoes, mini Crab Cakes (see p. 36), sautéed Polenta (see p. 19), or even a sautéed shrimp.

SERVES 4

4 sweet corn cobs

4 cups/1 liter cold milk

½ sweet onion, chopped

1 bunch thyme

1 sprig cilantro

1 leek, white part only, chopped

salt and pepper

chives or your favorite herb,
    finely chopped, for garnish

Remove and discard the husks and silks from the corn cobs. Roughly cut the corn from each cob, and place the kernels and cobs in a large stockpot. Add the milk, onion, thyme, and cilantro; simmer for 15 minutes.

Add the leek, season with salt and pepper, and cook for another 5 minutes. Purée, strain, and adjust seasoning.

Ladle the soup into warmed bowls. Sprinkle chopped chives or your favorite herb over top.

VICHYSSOISE

Potato and leek soup

Vichyssoise is the most used and abused French soup in the world. But do not judge it until you have made it properly. My approach is to honor both the traditions and the ingredients, bringing out the best in the potatoes and the leeks. Done right, the flavors will delicately complement each other. Try this recipe, and you will truly know your vichyssoise.

Serve this soup chilled, in shallow bowls. If you like, place a small scoop of Fingerling Potato Salad with Radishes (see p. 118) in the center. Finish with a sprinkle of chives. It can also be served hot, with a poached egg floating in the center.

SERVES 4

2 shallots, sliced

2 leeks, white part only, sliced

¼ cup/50 ml unsalted butter

3 medium Yukon Gold potatoes, peeled and cut into small dice

6 cups/1.5 liters water

1 bouquet garni (see p. 10)

⅔ cup/150 ml whipping cream

salt and pepper

In an uncovered skillet over low heat, cook the shallots and leeks gently in the butter until soft and translucent; do not allow them to color. Add the potatoes, water, and bouquet garni; simmer until tender, about 15 minutes. Remove the bouquet garni. Purée the soup using a hand blender. Add the cream; blend again. Season with salt and pepper.

SOUPE DE TOMATES PETIT DÉJEUNER

Breakfast tomato soup

Soup for breakfast? That is how my grandfather started every day. He fortified his with wine, but we're going to be a little more family-friendly and offer what is, but should not be, an unusual approach to a weekend breakfast.

SERVES 4

2 tbsp/30 ml olive oil

1 red onion, sliced

1 shallot, sliced

2 cloves garlic, germ removed, halved

2 lbs/1 kg ripe tomatoes, stemmed, cut into chunks

1 bouquet garni (see p. 10)

2 tbsp/30 ml honey

1 sprig basil

salt and pepper

2 tbsp/30 ml good-quality olive oil (optional)

6 cherry or grape tomatoes, halved (optional)

finely chopped chives, for garnish

Heat the olive oil in a heavy-bottomed pot. Sauté the onion and shallot gently for about 2 minutes or until slightly softened. Add the garlic; sauté for 1 minute. Add the tomatoes, bouquet garni, honey, and basil. Simmer gently for 30 minutes, seasoning with salt and pepper partway through the cooking. Remove the bouquet garni and basil.

Blend the soup in a blender or with a hand blender; strain. Stir in the olive oil, if using, for added richness and flavor. Adjust seasoning as needed.

Spoon a large ladleful of soup into warm bowls. Place a few halved grape tomatoes in the center and, if you like, drizzle with maltaise sauce (see p. 26) and sprinkle with chopped chives.

SOUPE À L'OIGNON GRATINÉE

French onion soup

Another bludgeoned French classic! Two common misconceptions that can take the joy out of what should be a fantastic dish are that the stock doesn't matter and that onions are just onions. Actually, it does and they aren't. The stock is the base of the flavor balance and should never be masked by the onions. And onions should be enjoyed for all their subtleties. Try it this way — you'll like it very much.

SERVES 4

2 tbsp/30 ml unsalted butter

4 large sweet onions, thinly sliced

1 tbsp/15 ml all-purpose flour

4 cups/1 liter chicken stock (see p. 10)
   or use store-bought

2 tbsp/30 ml brandy

2 tbsp/30 ml port

1 bouquet garni (see p. 10)

For topping:

1 baguette, sliced

1 clove garlic, halved

3 ½ oz/100 g Gruyère cheese, shredded

Heat the butter in a large stockpot over medium heat. Add the onions and cook to a light golden brown. Sprinkle in the flour; cook for 1 minute, stirring with a wooden spoon. Stir in the chicken stock, brandy, port, and bouquet garni. Gently simmer, covered, for 30 minutes.

To prepare the topping, rub the baguette slices with a cut side of garlic, top with the cheese.

Ladle the soup into warmed, heavy, ovenproof bowls and place a baguette slice on top. Place under the broiler until the cheese has melted and is slightly browned. Serve at once.

Salades et Sandwiches
Salads and Sandwiches

SALADE DE CREVETTES DE MATANES
À L'AVOCAT ET PAMPLEMOUSSE

Baby shrimp and grapefruit salad

The ingredients of this dish announce themselves as Mediterranean, and the freshness of the overall experience makes this a perfect summer salad. The flavor you get by making your mayonnaise and ketchup from scratch is always well worth the extra time.

SERVES 4

2 ruby red or pink grapefruit

2 medium avocados

2 tbsp/30 ml lemon vinaigrette (see p. 27)

7 oz/200 g cooked baby shrimp

½ cup/125 ml mayonnaise (see p. 21)
or use store-bought

2 tbsp/30 ml tomato ketchup (see p. 22)
or use store-bought

1 tbsp/15 ml brandy

1 hard-boiled egg

1 tbsp/15 ml finely chopped chives

Peel and segment the grapefruit, pat dry, and set aside. Halve the avocados; remove the skin and pits. Coat well with the lemon vinaigrette; set aside.

In a medium-sized bowl, combine the shrimp, mayonnaise, ketchup, and brandy. Stir in the grapefruit. Distribute half of the mixture among 4 plates. Place an avocado half on top of each, pitted side up; fill with remaining shrimp salad. Grate the hard-boiled egg over top, sprinkle with the chives, and serve. The salad can also be presented on one large serving plate, if desired.

SALADE D'ENDIVES AU GRUYÈRE
ET JAMBON

Belgian endive with Gruyère cheese and ham

Off the European continent, endive is the great undiscovered vegetable, but its hint of chicory makes it an interesting and appealing ingredient. When washing endive, use milk; water brings out the endive's bitterness.

Note: The endive may be prepared hours in advance. Immersing the cut endive leaves in milk prevents browning. The milk bath also slightly sweetens the endive's bitterness.

SERVES 4

6 Belgian endives

2 cups/500 ml milk

20 pecan halves

4 tbsp/60 ml diced Gruyère cheese

4 tbsp/60 ml diced cooked ham

½ cup/125 ml mustard dressing (see p. 28)

Cut the endive leaves off the root with a sharp knife. In a bowl, soak the leaves in the milk until ready to use. Pat dry before use.

In a skillet over medium heat, lightly toast the pecans (do not use any oil). Remove from heat and let cool.

In a bowl, toss the Gruyère cheese, ham, and endive with the mustard dressing and half of the toasted pecans. Distribute on individual plates, garnish with the remaining pecans, and serve at once.

SALADE COMPOSÉE AU MAÏS

Chopped salad with corn

Corn is a rare ingredient in France, but its sweetness works well in this dish, particularly with the cooked shiitake mushrooms.

SERVES 4

½ cup/125 ml shiitake mushrooms, stemmed

2 tbsp/30 ml olive oil

salt and pepper

1 head romaine lettuce

½ cup/125 ml fresh corn kernels

1 avocado, peeled, pitted, and diced

½ English or seedless cucumber, peeled and diced

1 cup/250 ml grape tomatoes, chopped

¼ cup/50 ml finely chopped roasted red peppers (see p. 24) or piquillo peppers

3–4 tbsp/45–60 ml yogurt dressing (see p. 27), for tossing

In a skillet over medium heat, sauté the mushrooms in the olive oil until soft and golden. Season with salt and pepper. Remove from heat; set aside to cool.

Remove the outer leaves of the romaine lettuce; put away for another use. Wash and shake dry the smaller, inner leaves.

In a bowl, combine the romaine lettuce, corn, avocado, cucumber, tomatoes, red peppers, and mushrooms. Toss with yogurt dressing. Serve at once.

SALADE LYONNAISE
AUX PETITS LARDONS

Dandelion and bacon salad with poached egg

In North America, the dandelion has long suffered for its reputation as a prolific weed. The French view it differently. There, people flock to the countryside in spring just to harvest the wild dandelion. This salad can be found in every restaurant in Lyon. *Note: You can make more or less sherry vinaigrette, as needed, by using a ratio of 1 part vinegar to 3 parts oil and adjusting the mustard to taste. Refrigerated, the dressing will keep for up to 1 week.*

SERVES 4

For sherry vinaigrette:

1 tbsp/15 ml sherry vinegar	1 shallot, minced
3 tbsp/45 ml grapeseed oil	1 tbsp/15 ml Dijon mustard

For salad:

2 oz/50 g pork belly (slab bacon)	4 eggs, poached, for garnish
1 blonde frisée	1 tbsp/15 ml finely chopped flat-leaf parsley
1 large bunch dandelion greens	1 tbsp/15 ml finely chopped chives
1 shallot, diced	

To make the sherry vinaigrette, whisk the sherry vinegar, grapeseed oil, shallot, and mustard together in a small bowl or vessel.

To make the salad, cut the bacon into approximately 1-inch (2.5 cm) pieces to make lardons.
Be sure each strip has a layer of both meat and fat.

Wash, dry, and trim the frisée and dandelion greens; mix together. Place a portion of the greens on each salad plate.

Blanch the bacon lardons in boiling water for 1 minute; drain. In a medium-sized skillet over medium heat, sauté the bacon to render a little fat. Add the shallot; cook until tender. Transfer the mixture to a plate; keep warm.

To deglaze the pan, pour in the sherry vinaigrette. With a wooden spoon or spatula, scrape up the bits of bacon and shallot left at the bottom of the skillet.

To assemble the salad, place hot poached eggs on the bed of greens; top with the bacon–shallot mixture and warm vinaigrette, and sprinkle with the parsley and chives.

SALADE D'HARICOTS VERTS

Green bean salad

My mother often prepared this salad for picnic lunches, and I have always loved it. The marinade robs the beans of some of their color but also draws out their flavor. Its freshness and zing is always a treat to the mouth.

SERVES 4

1 ³/₄ lbs/900 g French green beans

½ cup/125 ml mustard dressing (see p. 28)

1 clove garlic, germ removed, finely chopped

1 tbsp/15 ml finely chopped flat-leaf parsley

3 shallots, peeled and thinly sliced

salt and pepper

1 tsp/5 ml finely chopped chives

Cook the green beans in a large pot of boiling salted water for 3–5 minutes or until tender but not soft — the beans should hold their shape but not be too crunchy. Stop the cooking by plunging the beans into an ice-water bath for 2 minutes or just until cooled. Immediately remove from water, pat dry, and set aside.

In a large bowl, combine the mustard dressing, garlic and parsley. Gently toss in the beans and shallots. Let sit at room temperature or a cool place for 30 minutes.

To serve, season with salt and pepper; toss again gently. Top with a sprinkling of chopped chives.

SALADE D'HIVER AUX LÉGUMES RÔTIS

Roasted winter vegetable salad

In the winter, the choice of local produce may not be as great as in the summer, but you should never feel trapped by seasonal realities. This salad offers a taste of the season that is no less of a treat than the salad days of summer.

Toss with your favorite salad dressing and serve on a platter. For a meal, add a tomato or green salad. You can also use this dish as a base, topping it with fish or even lamb.

SERVES 4

2 tbsp/30 ml olive oil

1 bunch thyme

1 bunch flat-leaf parsley, finely chopped

pinch of ground ginger

pinch of cinnamon

salt and pepper

8 baby carrots, cut in half lengthwise

2 parsnips, cut in half lengthwise

1 white turnip, peeled, cut into 8 half-moon shapes

½ butternut squash, peeled, cut into 8 baton shapes

½ celery root, peeled, cut into 8 half-moon shapes

1 sweet potato, peeled, cut lengthwise into 8 pieces

1 red onion, sliced

Preheat oven to 400°F (200°C).

In a large bowl, combine the olive oil, thyme, parsley, ginger, cinnamon, and salt and pepper to taste. Gently toss the vegetables and sliced onion in the marinade to coat.

Spread the vegetables on a large baking sheet and roast for 20–30 minutes or until tender and golden brown. Serve warm or at room temperature.

SALADE VERTE AUX HERBES
"TOUTE SIMPLE"

"Grandma-style" mixed green salad

A salad can be simple or complex. Always, though, the quality of the ingredients will make all the difference. This is most true with the simplest of salads. With a mixed green salad, the freshness and the flavors must be given their chance to shine. This salad, lovely on its own, is an excellent accompaniment to potatoes.

SERVES 4

2 cloves garlic, germ removed, very finely chopped

4 tbsp/60 ml lemon vinaigrette (see p. 27)

1 head Boston bibb lettuce, torn into large pieces

1 handful mâche

1 head blonde frisée, trimmed into medium-sized pieces

1 head romaine lettuce heart, chopped

1 bunch chervil, leaves picked

2 tbsp/30 ml finely chopped flat-leaf parsley

2 tbsp/30 ml finely chopped chives

In a small bowl, combine the garlic and lemon vinaigrette; set aside.

Wash and assemble the Boston bibb lettuce, mâche, and frisée in a bowl. Remove the outer leaves of the romaine lettuce; reserve for another use. Wash and shake dry the smaller, inner leaves; chop and add to the bowl.

Toss the greens with the dressing and half of the herbs. Plate and sprinkle with the remaining herbs. Serve at once.

SALADE DE ROMAINE AUX
BAIES SÉCHÉES

Romaine and dried fruit salad

I make this salad primarily in the wintertime. The concentrated flavors of the dried fruits are a real treat, and, if you're a planner, drying the fruits yourself adds to the experience.

SERVES 4

2 heads romaine lettuce

2 Royal Gala apples

⅓ cup/75 ml ravigot dressing
   (see p. 25)

1 tbsp/15 ml dried cherries, halved

1 tbsp/15 ml dried blueberries

1 tbsp/15 ml dried cranberries, halved

Remove the outer leaves of the romaine lettuce; reserve for another use. Wash and shake dry the smaller, inner leaves. Dice the apples and gently toss together with the dressing and half of the dried fruit. Garnish with the remaining dried fruit. Serve at once.

SANDWICH DE CANARD MARINÉ
AUX CHAMPIGNONS

Grilled duck with marinated mushroom sandwich

When using barbecue duck as an ingredient, you are not likely to do better than picking one up in Chinatown.

For the marinated mushrooms, you will need to make a reasonable quantity to get the right flavor and texture. Use the leftovers as you would any good relish — as a condiment, in a sandwich with goat cheese, or even as a garnish. Place a little in the bottom of a soup bowl and ladle Cream of Button Mushroom Soup with Chanterelles (see p. 57) over top.

SERVES 4

For marinated mushrooms:

1 portobello mushroom, stemmed

4 shiitake mushrooms, stemmed

2 tbsp/30 ml olive oil

2 slices lemon

1 clove garlic

1 sprig thyme

For sandwiches:

½ barbecue duck

1 tbsp/15 ml mayonnaise (see p. 21) or use store-bought

1 tsp/5 ml chopped pickled ginger

4 tsp/20 ml unsalted butter

8 slices nine-grain bread

4 tsp/20 ml marinated mushrooms

To make the marinated mushrooms, remove the gills from the portobello mushroom with a teaspoon; discard. Finely chop the mushroom cap. Slice the shiitake mushrooms.

In a skillet over medium heat, sauté the mushrooms in a pan with about half of the olive oil, until lightly browned. Add the remaining olive oil, lemon, garlic, and thyme. Warm for 10 minutes; remove from heat, setting aside to cool and allow the oil to become infused with flavor. Pour the oil and mushroom mixture into a jar and refrigerate until ready to use.

To make the sandwiches, pull the duck meat off the bone; shred with a fork. In a bowl, mix together the duck meat, mayonnaise, and pickled ginger.

Butter the bread slices on both sides. Spread a layer of marinated mushrooms on 4 slices of bread; top with the duck mixture, and then another slice of bread. Grill the sandwich in a sandwich press, cast-iron pan, or nonstick pan, over medium heat until golden brown. Serve hot.

SANDWICH GRILLÉ AUX TROIS
FROMAGES ET BEURRE D'HERBES

Grilled three-cheese sandwich with herb butter

How can this staple be improved on? The answer, of course, lies in the cheese and the bread. With this sandwich, kids discover there's more to cheese than individually wrapped slices. Cut into bite-sized portions, these sandwiches make a great appetizer for grown-ups.

SERVES 4

For herb butter:

½ cup/125 ml unsalted
   butter, softened

1 tbsp/15 ml finely chopped
   flat-leaf parsley

1 tbsp/15 ml finely chopped chervil

salt and pepper

For sandwiches:

8 slices white sandwich bread

4 oz/115 g Ossau Irati cheese, sliced

4 oz/115 g Brie cheese, sliced

½ oz/15 g chèvre

To make the herb butter, combine the butter with the parsley, chervil, salt, and pepper in a small bowl. Butter both sides of the bread slices with the herb butter. Make a sandwich by layering an Ossau Irati cheese slice on the bottom, a Brie slice in the middle, and crumbled chèvre on top. In a nonstick pan, grill the sandwiches on both sides until the cheese softens and the bread is a toasted golden brown. Remove crusts, cut, and serve.

CROQUE MONSIEUR ET
CROQUE MADAME

Ham and cheese with béchamel sauce

This fast and simple lunch is a staple at bistros throughout France. It is easy to make, delicious, and so much more enjoyable than just bread and filling.

SERVES 4

2 tbsp/30 ml butter

8 slices egg bread

8 thin slices cooked ham

4 slices Gruyère cheese

2 cups/500 ml béchamel sauce (see p. 23)

7 oz/200 g Gruyère cheese, shredded

4 eggs (optional)

Butter the bread slices on both sides. Place 2 slices of ham and 1 slice of Gruyère cheese on each of four slices; top each with 2 tbsp/30 ml béchamel sauce and another slice of bread. Spread each sandwich with another 2 tbsp/30 ml of béchamel sauce and one-quarter of the shredded Gruyère. Grill under the broiler until the cheese is bubbly and lightly browned. For croque madame, fry 4 eggs in a nonstick skillet. Top the grilled sandwiches with one egg each. Serve at once.

PISSALADIÈRE AU SAUMON FRAIS

Pissaladière with onions and fresh salmon

This classic pizza-like open-face tart never fails to make an impression. A drizzle of Ravigot Dressing (see p. 25) adds color as well as a complex and delightful herb flavor. *Note: If you prefer not to make the dough from scratch, use 1 sheet store-bought puff pastry, rolled a few times to flatten the layers slightly. Don't over-roll the dough, as you want it to rise somewhat. The Savory Tart Pastry (see p. 14) will also work well.*

SERVES 4–6

For dough:

2 tsp/10 ml active dry yeast

1 ⅓ cups/325 ml all-purpose flour

1 tsp/5 ml sugar

1 tsp/5 ml salt

3 eggs

For topping:

4 tsp/20 ml extra virgin olive oil

1 lb/500 g yellow onions, thinly sliced

1 tsp/5 ml chopped fresh thyme

salt and pepper

4 tbsp/60 ml olive tapenade (see p. 22), or to taste

8–12 anchovy fillets

¼ cup/50 ml chopped olives (oil-packed Moroccan or black olive of your choice)

¾ lb/400 g salmon fillet, skinned, thinly sliced

4 tsp/20 ml extra virgin olive oil, for drizzling

1 tbsp/15 ml finely chopped flat-leaf parsley

To make the dough, dissolve the yeast in 1 tbsp/15 ml warm water. Sift the flour onto a work surface and make a well in the center. Add the salt and sugar to one side of the flour, building a small flour wall to keep them away from the well. Add the yeast mixture to the well, keeping it away from the salt.

Crack 2 of the eggs into the well and slowly, using your fingertips, work the eggs and yeast into the flour, now incorporating the sugar and salt. As you work your way around, draw in more of the flour. The dough should be soft, not sticky. Knead the dough until it is a consistent texture.

Put the dough into a lightly oiled (or lightly floured) stainless-steel bowl, cover with plastic wrap, and leave in a warm place to rise until double in size, about 1 hour. Punch the dough down, fold it over once, and rewrap it in the plastic wrap. Refrigerate until ready to use.

To make the topping, heat the olive oil in a skillet over low heat; gently sauté the onions until they are soft and translucent but not browned. Stir in the thyme and salt and pepper to taste; cook for 1 minute. Remove from heat and set aside.

Preheat the oven to 400°F (200°C).

Grease a large baking sheet. On a lightly floured surface, evenly roll out the dough to desired shape and place it on the baking sheet.

In a small bowl, combine the remaining egg with a pinch of salt and 2 tbsp/30 ml cold water to make an egg wash. Brush the egg wash on the outer ½-inch (1 cm) edge of the dough, to make a border.

Prick the bottom of the pastry in several places with a fork. Spread the olive tapenade on the dough in the center, leaving the borders untouched. Arrange the sautéed onion over top. Arrange the anchovy fillets in a criss-cross pattern over the onions and decoratively arrange the olives around the anchovies.

Bake for about 10 minutes. Remove from the oven. Place the sliced salmon on top. Bake for another 3–5 minutes or until the pastry edges are golden brown. Serve warm, drizzled with a little extra virgin olive oil and, if you like, a drizzle of ravigot dressing, along with a sprinkling of parsley.

PAN BAGNAT

Niçoise salad sandwich

Messy and juicy, this sandwich is very popular in the south of France. The dressing soaks into the bread, and the flavors are intense and pleasurable.

SERVES 4

3 ½ oz/100 g French green beans

2 vine-ripened tomatoes,
  cut into pieces or sliced

2 fingerling potatoes, boiled,
  skins on, thinly sliced

1 roasted red pepper, skinned
  and chopped (see p. 24)

2 shallots, diced

1–2 cloves garlic, crushed

24 black olives, pitted and halved

4 anchovy fillets

2 hard-boiled eggs, sliced

1 tbsp/15 ml finely chopped
  flat-leaf parsley

1 tbsp/15 ml finely chopped chives

1 sprig small-leafed basil,
  leaves picked

salt and pepper

¼ cup/50 ml olive oil

4 large brioche or milk-bread rolls

4 leaves butter lettuce

Snap off the stem ends of the beans. Blanch the beans in a large pot of rapidly boiling salted water. Cook until tender-crisp, about 2–3 minutes. Immediately immerse in an ice-water bath to stop the cooking. Drain and pat dry. Slice lengthwise.

In a large bowl, gently toss together all ingredients except the bread and lettuce. Let stand at room temperature for 30 minutes, for flavors to blend.

Slice the brioches or rolls, place 2–3 spoonfuls of the marinated salad on the bottom half of the bread, add a piece of lettuce for color, and cover with the top half of the bread.

Serve the sandwiches with cutlery, as the moist filling will soak into the bread.

Oeufs et Fromages
Eggs and Cheese

OEUFS COCOTTE, PURÉE DE
TOMATE ET TOMME

Coddled eggs with tomato and Tomme de Savoie cheese

This dish is cooked in one- or two-egg-sized ramekins. It is simple to make, and you can add any flavoring you like, such as shredded cheese or tomato sauce, or even a small slice of ham, placed at the bottom. Tomme de Savoie cheese is available in most cheese shops.

SERVES 2–4

3 tbsp/45 ml unsalted butter

3 ½ oz/100 g Tomme de Savoie
   cheese, shredded

4 tbsp/60 ml tomato sauce
   (smooth, not chunky)

salt and pepper

4 eggs

Preheat oven to 325°F (160°C).

Butter the inside of four 1-egg- or two 2-egg-sized ramekins. Sprinkle the Tomme de Savoie cheese inside each. Distribute the tomato sauce among the ramekins. Season with salt and pepper. Crack the eggs on top of the tomato sauce, being careful not to break the yolks. Season again to taste.

Set the ramekins in a deep ovenproof skillet or roasting pan; add hot water to the skillet or pan to two-thirds up the outsides of the ramekins. Bake for 5–7 minutes or until the whites are just set. Don't overcook: the ramekins hold their heat, so the dish will continue cooking for 1–2 minutes once removed from the oven.

Serve in the ramekins.

OMELETTE AU CHABICHOU
ET HERBES FRAÎCHES

Folded omelet with Chabichou cheese and fresh herbs

Chabichou is a goat cheese from the Poitiers region in France's south Loire Valley. At maturity this cheese has a sweet, goaty taste, but its finish is tangy and slightly salty — an ideal balance of flavors to elevate any omelet. Here, parsley and chervil complement the herbaceous quality of the cheese. Chabichou is readily available in cheese shops.

SERVES 4

7 oz/200 g chilled Chabichou

8 eggs

⅓ cup/75 ml milk

2 sprigs flat-leaf parsley,
   leaves finely chopped

4 sprigs chervil, leaves picked

salt and pepper

2 tbsp/30 ml unsalted butter

butter, for brushing

8 chives, finely chopped

While the cheese is cold, cut it into eight ¼-inch (5 mm) slices; set aside to bring to room temperature.

In a bowl, gently mix together the eggs, milk, about half of the chopped parsley and one-quarter of the chervil, and salt and pepper to taste.

Over medium heat, melt the butter in a nonstick skillet wide enough for the omelet to lie flat. When the butter starts to bubble, add the egg mixture and stir gently with a wooden spoon for 1 minute. Stop stirring and let the egg cook for another minute.

Tip the pan to allow any uncooked egg to run to the side of the pan. Continue cooking just until the omelet is lightly set. Place the cheese in a single layer on top of the egg, covering half the omelet. Fold the omelet by tipping the pan away from you. Gently loosen the sides, flipping the top edge over with a spatula or wooden spoon.

Finish by brushing the omelet with butter to add a shine; sprinkle with the remaining parsley and chervil, and the chopped chives.

OEUFS BROUILLÉS AUX
TRUFFES NOIRES

Scrambled eggs with black truffle

Certain simple foods allow the singularity of their ingredients to come through, creating a beautiful balance to the complexities you find elsewhere. With eggs, the opportunity is always to present a story of delicate subtleties, but care must always be taken not to overpower the flavor of the eggs. Fresh truffle transforms everyday scrambled eggs into haute cuisine. Other flavors that work well with eggs are smoked salmon, asparagus, and ham; these can be added part way through the cooking process, when the eggs are still creamy. Many chopped fresh herbs are also wonderful with eggs and can be added directly to the raw eggs. I would suggest starting with the basics, then experimenting with the tastes that appeal to you and are locally available.

SERVES 4

12 medium eggs

salt and pepper

¼ cup/50 ml unsalted butter

1 tbsp/15 ml whipping cream

2 tsp/10 ml shaved black truffle

In a large bowl, gently beat the eggs. Season with salt and pepper.

Melt the butter in the upper pot of a double boiler (or in a metal bowl placed over hot, simmering water). Add the eggs and cook very gently, stirring constantly with a whisk or wooden spoon. Scrape the eggs up from the bottom of the pan as they start to cook, gently mixing them back into the still-uncooked eggs. When the eggs start to cook and become creamy, stir in the cream. Remove the eggs from the heat (they will continue to cook), stirring constantly until desired texture is achieved. Stir in the truffle. Serve at once.

TARTELETTE AU CHÈVRE ET
ÉCHALOTES CONFITES

Goat-cheese tart with caramelized shallots

Sometimes it's fun to treat people to a blast of flavor. Without fail, those who taste this dish open their eyes a little wider in surprise and appreciation. It's all about balancing the strong but complementary flavors to create a third, unique sensation. These tarts go well with slices of tomato or a green salad.

SERVES 4 (eight 4-inch (10 cm) tartlets or one 9-inch (23 cm) tart)

9 oz/250 g savory tart pastry (see p. 14) or 1 sheet store-bought puff pastry

2 large shallots, sliced

2 tbsp/30 ml sugar

⅓ cup/75 ml Banyuls or balsamic vinegar

4 oz/115 g chèvre, softened

½–1 cup/125–250 ml royale mixture (see p. 17), or enough to fill tarts to two-thirds

1 tbsp/15 ml finely chopped chives

Prepare tart pastry and blind bake (see p. 14).

In a heavy-bottomed saucepan, bring the shallots, sugar, and vinegar to a boil; reduce heat and simmer gently until the pan is almost dry. Remove from heat and let cool.

Distribute the shallot reduction among tart shells. Crumble equal amounts of chèvre into each tart shell. Pour in the royale mixture, filling the tart shells to about two-thirds. Don't overfill — you should be able to see some of the cheese.

Bake in a 350°F (180°C) oven for 8–10 minutes or until the royale mixture is firm and the pastry is a pale golden brown. Bake a single large tart for 10–15 minutes. Sprinkle with the chives and serve.

TARTE DE POIREAUX AU BRIE

Leek and Brie tart

Both leeks and Brie are staples of northern France, making this dish a typically Parisian lunch item. Some say leeks are the poor man's asparagus, but this dish proves that wonderful flavor is not restricted by budget.

SERVES 4 (eight 4-inch (10 cm) tartlets or one 9-inch (23 cm) tart)

9 oz/250 g savory tart pastry (see p. 14) or 1 sheet store-bought puff pastry

2 large shallots, diced

1 leek, white and light green part only, sliced

¼ cup/50 ml unsalted butter

salt and pepper

14 oz/400 g Brie cheese, rind on, sliced

1 cup/250 ml royale mixture (see p. 17), or enough to fill tarts to two-thirds

finely chopped chives, for garnish

Prepare tart pastry and blind bake (see p. 14). Reduce oven temperature to 325°F (160°C).

In an uncovered nonstick skillet over low heat, cook the shallots and leeks gently in the butter until soft and translucent; do not allow to color. Season the cooked leeks and shallots with salt and pepper; transfer to the warm tart shell. Place slices of Brie on top of the leeks and shallots. Pour in the royale mixture, filling the tart shell to about two-thirds.

Bake a single large tart for 10–15 minutes or until the royale mixture is firm, and the pastry is a pale golden brown. Bake smaller tarts for 8–10 minutes. Garnish with a sprinkling of chopped chives.

QUICHE LORRAINE ET
JAMBON DE BAYONNE

Quiche Lorraine with Bayonne ham

In this case, my way of making this classic quiche is very close to the traditional way, with particular care given to finding the freshest and best ingredients. The differences lie in my choice of Emmental cheese, the inclusion of onions, and the addition of ham. This quiche goes well with a mixed green salad.

SERVES 4 (eight 4-inch (10 cm) tartlets or one 9-inch (23 cm) tart)

9 oz/250 g savory tart pastry (see p. 14)
   or 1 sheet store-bought puff pastry

½ lb/250 g slab bacon (pork belly)

½ onion, chopped

salt and pepper

3 ½ oz/100 g Emmental cheese,
   finely shredded

1 cup/250 ml royale mixture (see p. 17),
   or enough to fill tart to two-thirds

3 ½ oz/100 g Bayonne ham, sliced

Prepare the tart pastry and blind bake (see p. 14).

Cut bacon into approximately 1-inch (2.5 cm) strips to make lardons, with a layer of meat and fat in each. Blanch the bacon in boiling water for 1 minute.

In a nonstick pan over medium-low heat, gently sauté the bacon to render a little fat. Add the onion to the pan; cook gently until soft and translucent. Season with salt and pepper. Drain off the excess fat.

Toss the Emmental cheese with the bacon–onion mixture and spread onto the baked tart shells. Pour in the royale mixture to fill tarts to two-thirds. Bake in a 350°F (180°C) oven for 8–10 minutes or until pale golden brown. If using one large tart shell, bake for 10–15 minutes or until pale golden brown.

Serve hot or at room temperature, with several slices of Bayonne ham arranged on top of each quiche.

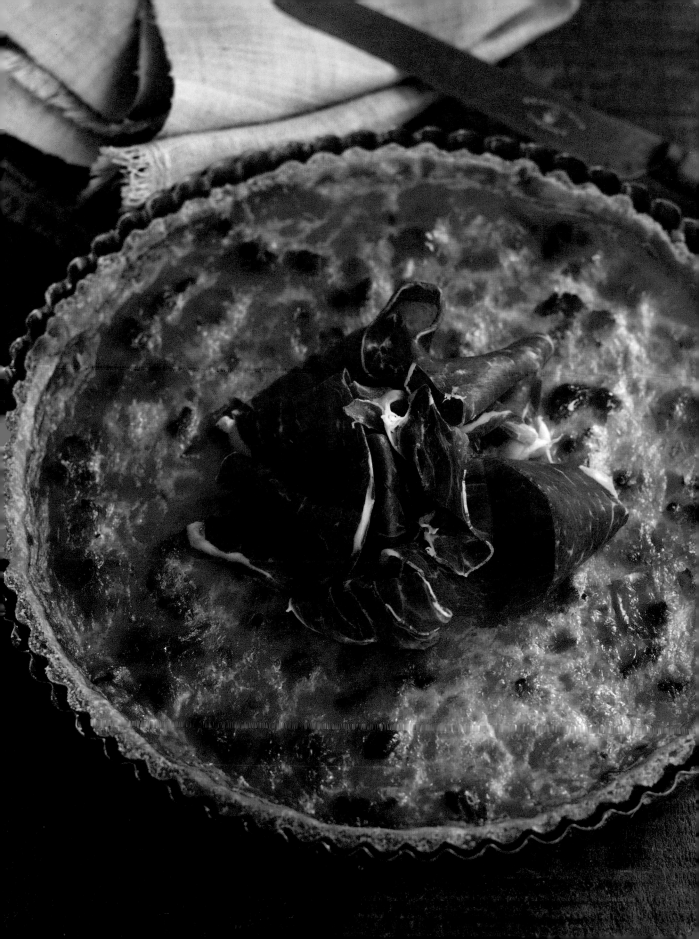

OEUFS POCHÉS ET POTIRON RÔTI

Poached eggs with roasted butternut squash

Perfect for an autumn Sunday brunch, this dish makes a bold visual statement. The orange hues in sharp contrast to the egg white make for a sunny, cheerful meal. The rich creamy egg yolk acts as a sauce, but the dish also works very well with the addition of a hollandaise or Maltaise Sauce (see p. 26). Or you could simply serve it with a green salad and crusty baguette.

Note: The squash can be tossed with the marinade and stored in the refrigerator, covered, up to 1 day in advance.

SERVES 4

1 butternut squash

2 tbsp/30 ml olive oil

2 tbsp/30 ml orange juice

1 tsp/5 ml maple syrup

1 sprig thyme

½ cinnamon stick
  (or pinch of ground cinnamon)

salt and pepper

1 tsp/5 ml lemon juice

4 eggs

Preheat oven to 350°F (180°C).

Peel, seed, and thickly slice the squash.

In a small bowl, blend the olive oil, orange juice, maple syrup, thyme, cinnamon, and salt and pepper to taste. In a baking dish, toss the squash with the marinade. Roast the squash until soft and golden, 10–20 minutes.

In a medium-sized pot, bring 2 cups/500 ml of water and the lemon juice to a very gentle simmer. Add the eggs gently, one by one. Poach for 3 minutes.

Meanwhile, place the cooked squash on a warm serving plate. Remove the eggs from the water with a slotted spoon and arrange on top of the squash. Serve at once.

TARTE AU POIRE AU COMTÉ

Bartlett pear with Comté cheese

Comté cheese has a complex nutty and caramelized flavor that's perfect for the sweetness of the pear. It is available in most cheese shops.

SERVES 4

4 ½ oz/125 g savory tart pastry
   (see p. 14) or ½ sheet store-bought
   puff pastry

½ cup/125 ml whole raw almonds

½ cup/125 ml ice wine

2 pears, ripe but firm, peeled, cored,
   halved lengthwise

3 tbsp/45 ml cream cheese, softened

1 sprig thyme, leaves picked

7 oz/200 g Comté cheese, shredded

Preheat the oven to 350°F (180°C).

Roll out the pastry dough. Using a 4-inch (10 cm) pastry ring, cut out 4 circles. Prick the pastry circles with a fork several times. Bake on a parchment paper-lined baking sheet for 8–10 minutes or until golden brown. Cool, reserving the pan for later use. Change the parchment if greasy.

Toast the almonds on a baking sheet in the oven until lightly browned. Cool, then grind in a food processor, leaving the nuts somewhat chunky.

In a skillet over medium heat, heat the ice wine. Add the pears and poach at a very gentle simmer, with the lid on, turning them often with a spatula. Poach until cooked through, 5-10 minutes. Transfer to a plate; let cool cut-side down. Once cool, slice and fan the pears by making several vertical slices through the body of the pear, while preserving the connection at the stem end.

Place the pastry circles on a parchment paper-lined baking sheet. In a bowl, combine the cream cheese, thyme, and almonds. Spread in the center of each pastry circle. Place half a pear on top of each. Sprinkle with shredded Comté cheese.

Bake for 5 minutes or until the cheese is warm. Serve at once.

CRÊPE AU FROMAGE DE CHÈVRE

Savory goat-cheese crepe

This crepe is excellent as an appetizer or a canapé — the difference is simply a matter of serving size, with the smallest of crepes folding into bite-sized morsels.

SERVES 4 (2 crepes each as an appetizer, 16 canapés, or 24 mini canapés)

8 crepes (see p. 18)

2 shallots, minced

1 clove garlic, finely chopped

1 tbsp/15 ml unsalted butter

3 ½ oz/100 g chèvre, softened

1 tbsp/15 ml olive oil

1 tbsp/15 ml finely chopped chives

1 tbsp/15 ml finely chopped
   flat-leaf parsley

salt and pepper

Prepare the crepes according to the recipe.

Preheat oven to 325°F (160°C).

In an uncovered skillet over low heat, cook the shallots and garlic gently in the butter until soft and translucent; do not allow to color. In a bowl, combine the chèvre, shallots, and garlic. Add the olive oil, stirring until creamy. Stir in the chives and parsley. Season with salt and pepper.

Spread a spoonful of filling on a quarter of a crepe. Fold in half and then in half again to form a triangle. Fill the remaining crepes. Bake for 2 minutes to reheat the crepes and warm the cheese. Serve at once.

FONDUE AU FROMAGE

Cheese fondue

The secret to a successful fondue is in knowing that the pleasure lies as much in the ceremony as in the flavors. It's fun for a group, it's romantic for a couple. A cheese fondue is a very forgiving dish, and its rules are simple: three cheeses and Kirsch.

SERVES 4

7 oz/200 g Comté cheese

7 oz/200 g Emmental cheese

7 oz/200 g Beaufort cheese

2 cups/500 ml dry white wine

2 cloves garlic

½ cup/125 ml Kirsch

freshly ground black pepper

1 loaf challah or egg bread

1 Granny Smith apple (unpeeled)

Shred or thinly slice the three cheeses. Place the cheeses, wine, and garlic in a heavy-bottomed pot; heat over medium heat until the cheese is completely melted. Pour in the Kirsch, stirring to mix. Season with pepper.

In the meantime, cut the bread into bite-sized cubes and slice the apple, for dipping.

Transfer the cheese mixture to a fondue pot. Serve immediately.

SOUFFLÉ AU FROMAGE

Cheese soufflé

Do not be afraid of soufflés. The trick is simply to be meticulous. The temperature is the temperature. The ingredients are the ingredients. The method is the method. Separately they are simple. Bringing the elements together is just a matter of care and attention. Try it out on your family first. Confidence comes with success and, in this case, success comes surprisingly easily.

SERVES 4

5 oz/150 g Comté cheese, shredded, plus more for serving (optional)

1 ¾ cups/425 ml béchamel sauce (see p. 23)

4 eggs, separated

salt and pepper

1 tbsp/15 ml butter

pinch of salt

juice of ½ lemon

In a medium-sized bowl, stir together the Comté cheese and béchamel sauce. Beat in the egg yolks one by one. Season with salt and pepper. Cool the mixture in the refrigerator.

Adjust the oven rack to accommodate a risen soufflé — the lower center rack is usually fine. Preheat the oven to 400°F (200°C).

Butter a 6-cup/1.5 liter soufflé dish or individual ramekins. Keep refrigerated until needed.

In a large bowl, whisk the egg whites with a pinch of salt until stiff peaks form. Slowly beat until the whites are fluffy and glossy, stirring in the lemon juice a little at a time. Gently fold a quarter of the egg whites into the cheese–egg mixture; gently fold that mixture back into the remaining egg whites.

Pour the mixture into the prepared dish, filling to the top. Tap the dish hard on the countertop several times to get rid of any air bubbles. Smooth the surface with a pallet knife or spatula. Use a clean, dry cloth to wipe off any excess egg mixture from the rim and sides of the dish, then gently run the point of a knife around the edge, to break the surface tension — this will allow the soufflé to rise more easily.

Bake a single large soufflé for 15 minutes; bake individual ramekins for 5 minutes. Reduce temperature to 350°F (180°C). Keeping the oven closed, cook for another 5 minutes or until the soufflé is puffed and light brown on top. Serve at once, sprinkled with shredded cheese, if desired.

TARTE À L'OIGNON AU
CROTTIN DE CHAVIGNOL

Onion tart with Crottin de Chavignol cheese

Chavignol is a small village near Sancerre in the north-central Loire region of France, where they have been breeding and milking goats since the sixteenth century. So it follows that they know their cheese! In this recipe, I balance the sharpness of the cheese with the sweet tang of onions for a flavor sensation that guarantees a response.

Serve as an appetizer, with veal or chicken.

SERVES 4 (sixteen 2-inch (5 cm) tartlets or one 9-inch (23 cm) tart)

9 oz/250 g savory tart pastry (see p. 14)
   or 1 sheet store-bought puff pastry

½ cup/125 ml unsalted butter

4 Spanish or other sweet onions,
   finely chopped

2 eggs

½ cup/125 ml Devon cream
   or 45% cream

salt and pepper

2 tsp/10 ml truffle oil (optional)

5 oz/150 g Crottin de Chavignol cheese,
   cut into 8 slices

Prepare the pastry and blind bake (see p. 14).

Melt the butter in a skillet over low heat and very gently fry the onions for about 30 minutes, turning frequently, until soft but not colored. Remove from heat and set aside to cool.

In a bowl, mix together the onions, eggs, and cream. Season with salt and pepper. Stir in the truffle oil, if using.

Pour the filling into the tart shells, filling to about two-thirds. Bake the tarts for 8–10 minutes or until the filling has set. Bake a single large tart for 10–15 minutes. Remove from the oven, top each tartlet with a slice of Crottin de Chavignol cheese, and bake for another 5 minutes or until the cheese is warm.

TATINS D'ENDIVES AU FROMAGE
ET NOIX DE PECANES

Belgian endive tatins with Gruyère cheese and pecans

In this recipe, the tatin "crust" is made of endive leaves. Beyond the wonderful balance of textures and flavors, these tatins plate with a flair that is always satisfying.

SERVES 4

6 Belgian endives

2 cups/500 ml whole milk

16 pecan halves

3 tbsp/45 ml unsalted butter

2 oranges, 1 juiced, 1 segmented

1 tbsp/15 ml honey

salt and pepper

7 oz/200 g Gruyère cheese, diced

1 sprig tarragon, finely chopped

Slice the endives at their bases, removing the leaves. Soak them in the milk for 1 hour. Remove from the milk and pat dry.

Preheat the oven to 350°F (180°C).

Toast the pecans on a baking sheet until light brown.

Melt the butter in a large skillet over medium heat. Stir in the orange juice and honey. Add the endives, and salt and pepper to taste. Cook until the endives soften, about 5 minutes.

Cover a baking sheet with parchment paper. Place four 3½-inch (9 cm) pastry rings (no bottom) on top.

Working your way around the ring, carefully arrange the endive leaves to form a bottom within each ring, overlapping the sides so that the leaves will fold into the center to seal the tarts once they are filled.

Fill the bottom of the tarts with the orange segments, Gruyère cheese, tarragon, and pecans. Fold the ends of the endive leaves over to make the top "crust." Bake for 15 minutes or until the leaves are lightly browned.

Use a palette knife or spatula to support the tart and flip it upside down for serving. Gently remove the ring and serve warm.

TOMATES DE VIGNE AU SAINTE MAURE

Roasted tomatoes with Sainte Maure cheese

Heating a tomato always brings out its flavor. Here the cheese is a perfect accent. The simplicity and ease with which this dish is prepared will make the compliments feel undeserved, but there is a power in simplicity. I like to serve this right when tomatoes come into season.

This dish is very versatile — it works equally well served as a warm appetizer on a bed of salad greens or as a side course to fish or chicken.

SERVES 4

4 vine-ripened tomatoes, halved

¼ cup/50 ml olive oil

1 shallot, finely diced

1 clove garlic, chopped

½ lb/250 g Sainte Maure cheese,
    cut into 8 slices

1 tsp/5 ml finely chopped chervil

1 tsp/5 ml finely chopped chives

1 tsp/5 ml finely chopped thyme

warmed olive oil, for drizzling

Preheat the oven to 300°F (150°C).

In an ovenproof dish, gently toss together the tomatoes, olive oil, shallots, and garlic. Bake for 5 minutes — just long enough to warm the ingredients and bring out the flavors. Flip each tomato cut-side up; top each with a slice of cheese. Bake 1 minute to soften the cheese slightly. Remove from the oven, sprinkle with the herbs, drizzle warm olive oil over top, and serve in the baking dish.

Pommes de Terre
Potatoes

POMMES ANNA

Potatoes Anna

Plating and presentation are always important in French cooking. Here is an opportunity to start with a classic French dish, then open it up for a twist. The warm potatoes with the fresh salad look great together and taste even better. Serve the potatoes warm with Dandelion and Bacon Salad with Poached Egg (see p. 74) or lardons in the center.

SERVES 4

1 ½ lbs/750 g Yukon Gold potatoes, uniform in size (peeling optional)

½ cup/125 ml unsalted butter

salt and pepper

Preheat oven to 350°F (180°C).

With a mandolin, cut the potatoes into very thin, uniform slices. Do not rinse. Transfer to a bowl.

In an 8- or 10-inch (20 or 25 cm) cast-iron or ovenproof skillet over medium heat, melt the butter.

Toss the potatoes with the butter. Season with salt and pepper.

Arrange the potatoes around the outer edge of the skillet, overlapping the slices as you work your way around, creating even layers. Alternatively, create a ring by leaving a space in the center of the potatoes for a garnish.

Cover the skillet with tin foil and bake for about 40 minutes or until the potatoes are tender. Remove the foil and bake for another 10 minutes or until the bottom layer of potatoes are golden brown. Pour off any excess butter. Place a plate on top of the skillet and invert quickly to transfer the potatoes intact. Serve warm.

SALADE DE RATTES AUX RADIS

Fingerling potato salad with radishes

I have found that people can get very competitive with their potato salads. Potatoes actually have much more flavor than you might expect. Fingerling potatoes are harvested young, and their sweetness is undeniable.

SERVES 4

2 lbs/1 kg fingerling potatoes

4 red radishes, sliced

1 shallot, finely diced

1 bunch chervil, fronds plucked

2 mint leaves, very thinly sliced

1 tbsp/15 ml finely chopped chives

1 tbsp/15 ml chopped flat-leaf parsley

¼ cup/50 ml mayonnaise (see p. 21) or use store-bought

¼ cup/50 ml mustard dressing (see p. 28)

2 hard-boiled eggs, sliced

In a large pot of cold, salted water, bring the unpeeled potatoes to a gentle boil; cook until tender. Drain and let cool. Once cooled, cut into ¼-inch- (5 mm) thick slices.

In a large bowl, toss the potatoes with the radishes, shallot, half of the chervil, mint, chives, parsley, mayonnaise, and mustard dressing. Add the eggs, tossing gently.

Serve at room temperature, sprinkled with the remaining chervil.

TARTE AUX POMMES DE TERRE

Potato tart

It is unusual to think of potatoes with pastry, but it is this kind of mixing of tastes and textures that gives French cuisine its distinction. It is always a matter of considering how one flavor might create a context for the presentation of another. In this case the result is superb.

Serve the tart in wedges. For a heartier meal, accompany with a few slices of pork sausage and a mixed green salad.

SERVES 4

18 oz/500 g savory tart pastry (see p. 14)
  or 2 sheets store-bought puff pastry

2 lbs/1 kg Yukon Gold potatoes,
  peeled, very thinly sliced

1 onion, sliced

1 tbsp/15 ml butter

1 cup/250 ml royale mixture (see p. 17)

2 tbsp/30 ml finely chopped chives

1 egg

pinch of salt

Divide the tart pastry in two; reserve half. Prepare the other half in a 9-inch (23 cm) tart pan; blind bake (see p. 14).

In the meantime, in a large pot of boiling salted water, cook the potatoes for 2 minutes; set aside to cool.

In an uncovered skillet over medium-low heat, cook the onion gently in butter until soft and translucent, but not colored. Remove from heat and let cool.

In a large bowl, mix the royale mixture, potatoes, onion, and chives. Fill the tart shell (while it's still warm) with the mixture, arranging the potatoes in loose layers.

Roll out the remaining pastry; cover the tart, making a vent in the top to allow steam to escape.

In a small bowl, combine the egg with a pinch of salt and 2 tbsp/30 ml cold water to make an egg wash. Brush the top of the tart with the egg wash. Bake for about 30 minutes or until the tart is a medium golden brown.

GRATIN DAUPHINOIS

Dauphinois potatoes

This dish is typical of Lyon, and is very much like scalloped potatoes, but without the cheese. The cheeses of the Lyon region do not bake well, but the simplicity of the baked layered potatoes is beautiful. The trick to this recipe is to work quickly, as the potatoes begin to discolor once exposed to air.

SERVES 4

1 clove garlic, halved

¼ cup/50 ml unsalted butter

2 lbs/1 kg Yukon Gold
    potatoes, peeled

3 eggs

2 cups/500 ml whipping cream

salt and pepper

Preheat oven to 300°F (150°C).

Rub an 8-inch (20 cm) cast-iron skillet or ovenproof dish well with the garlic and butter.

Slice the potatoes very thinly with a mandolin. Rinse under cold water; pat dry.

In a large bowl, lightly beat together the eggs, cream, and salt and pepper to taste. Toss the potatoes in the mixture to coat. Transfer the potatoes and liquid to the pan. Bake for about 1 hour or until a light golden brown.

POMMES DE TERRE AU CITRON

Lemon potatoes

This is a very simple version of baked potatoes in which the flavors are given a kick with the simple citrus zing.

SERVES 4

2 lemons

½ cup/125 ml unsalted butter, softened

1 sprig thyme, finely chopped

4 medium Yukon Gold potatoes, peeled

1 lb/500 g rock or kosher salt

Preheat oven to 350°F (180°C).

Zest 1 lemon, then juice it. Cut the other lemon into 8 thin slices, discarding the ends. In a small bowl, blend together the butter, lemon zest, and thyme.

Cut a sliver from the bottom of each potato so it sits flat. Carefully make 3 or 4 vertical incisions into the potato, cutting down about half way. Being careful not to split the potato, use a knife to slide a little of the butter mixture into each incision.

Place 2 slices of lemon on top of each potato and wrap individually in aluminum foil. Keeping the potatoes upright, place them on a small baking sheet lined with rock or kosher salt, to raise the potatoes off the baking surface. Bake for 25–30 minutes or until the potatoes are fork-tender.

POMMES DE TERRE TARTIFLETTE

Potatoes gratin

This winter dish hails from Savoy, where their cheese has a wonderful history. In the thirteenth century, the farmers were taxed a percentage of their milk production. To avoid paying too much of their yield, they would hold back on some of the milking until after the collectors had passed. This interruption changed the quality of the remaining milk and the cheese made from it. "Reblochon" literally means "milk again."

SERVES 4

2 lbs/1 kg potatoes, peeled,
   sliced ½ inch (1 cm) thick

7 oz/200 g slab bacon (pork belly)

1 onion, sliced

butter, for coating baking dish

4 tbs/60 ml crème fraîche or
   Devon cream

salt and pepper

7 oz/200 g Reblochon cheese, shredded

Preheat oven to 325°F (160°C).

In a large pot of boiling salted water, cook the potatoes for 1 minute. Drain and set aside.

Cut the bacon into approximately 1-inch (2.5 cm) pieces to make lardons, with a layer of both meat and fat in each. In a skillet over medium heat, cook the bacon to render a little fat. Add the onions, and cook until a very light golden.

Butter an 8- or 9-inch (20 or 25 cm) ovenproof dish. Arrange the potatoes in overlapping layers; cover with the crème fraîche. Top with the onions and bacon. Season with salt and pepper. Sprinkle the cheese evenly on top.

Bake for about 15 minutes or until the potatoes are tender and the cheese golden.

POMMES DE TERRE SARLADAISES

Potatoes cooked in duck fat

This is another way to take potatoes to a higher level. Traditional in the southwest of France, it is a lighter, less greasy approach than you might expect.

Note: Duck fat is available at specialty food stores and some butchers. It will keep in a sealed container in the refrigerator for about 1 month.

SERVES 4

2 lbs/1 kg Yukon Gold potatoes, peeled, sliced ½ inch (1 cm) thick

4 oz/115 g duck fat

4 cloves garlic, germ removed, chopped

salt and pepper

1 tbsp/15 ml finely chopped flat-leaf parsley

Rinse the potatoes and pat dry.

Using a pastry cutter, cut potatoes into coins about 2 inches (5 cm) in diameter.

In a wide, heavy-bottomed skillet, heat the duck fat over medium heat to about 330°F (165°C).

Sauté the potatoes until lightly golden, flip and cook the other side. A few minutes before the potatoes are cooked through, stir in the garlic. Continue to cook until tender.

Remove the potatoes from the pan, drain on paper towel, and season with salt and pepper. Sprinkle with parsley and serve immediately.

POMMES SAVOYARDE

Scalloped potatoes in chicken broth with cheese

In the winter, when garden vegetables are less plentiful, this is a nice treat and an easy way to do gratinée potatoes. The broth reduces with the cheese to produce a sauce that is not unlike scalloped potatoes.

SERVES 4

2 lbs/1 kg Yukon Gold potatoes

2 tbsp/30 ml unsalted butter

salt and pepper

½ cup/125 ml chicken stock (see p. 10) or use store-bought

11 oz/300 g Gruyère cheese, roughly shredded

Preheat oven to 350°F (180°C).

Using a mandolin or sharp knife, slice potatoes about ½ inch (1 cm) thick. Rinse and pat dry. Butter the bottom of a baking dish. Season the potatoes with salt and pepper; layer the slices, overlapping, in the dish. Pour the stock over top. Top with the Gruyère cheese. Bake 20–25 minutes or until the potatoes are fork-tender.

Les Plats
Main Courses

CASSOULET

Navy bean stew with duck confit and sausages

The people around Toulouse grew up with this dish. Traditionally, it is weighted in favor of lamb, but the best mix is a matter of personal taste. When serving, it's all about inviting your family or guests to dig in. This warm, rustic dish is perfect for fall and winter. Serve at the table in the baking dish with fresh bread and a winter salad, if desired.

Note: Pork skin can be found at butcher shops and some specialty food shops.

SERVES 8

2 lbs/1 kg dry white navy beans

1 lb/500 g pork belly
 (slab bacon), halved

4 vine-ripened tomatoes,
 peeled and seeded

2 large onions, halved

1 carrot

1 head garlic, unpeeled, halved

1 large bouquet garni (see p. 10)

1 ¼ cups/300 ml beef broth

2 tbsp/30 ml duck fat

4 coarse pork sausages

4 veal sausages

1 large garlic sausage

4 duck confit legs (see p. 13)

7 oz/200 g pork skin (sheets)

2 cups/500 ml breadcrumbs

3 tbsp/45 ml flat-leaf parsley, leaves only

In a large, heavy-bottomed pot, cover the beans with cold unsalted water. Bring the beans to a boil; strain. Return the beans to the pot, cover with fresh cold water, add the pork belly, tomatoes, onions, carrot, garlic, and bouquet garni. Bring to a boil, then reduce heat to a simmer.

Heat the beef broth and keep on hand, using as needed to keep the beans moist during cooking. Brown the sausages in half of the duck fat; drain and set aside. When the beans are just beginning to soften, after about 2 hours, remove the pork belly, onions, carrot, garlic, and bouquet garni; discard. Add the sausages and duck legs; cook another 30 minutes or until the beans are tender.

Preheat oven to 300°F (150°C).

In a small pot, slightly heat the remaining duck fat.

Line the bottom and halfway up the sides of a clay baking dish or ovenproof casserole dish with the pork skin. Spoon in a layer of beans. Slice larger sausages into chunks and add, creating a middle layer of meat; cover with another layer of beans. In a mini food processor, combine the parsley and breadcrumbs. Sprinkle evenly over top. Drizzle with the warm duck fat.

Bake for 1 hour, releasing the steam every 15 minutes by breaking the crust that forms with a knife.

RATATOUILLE "BAYALDI"

Ratatouille "bayaldi"

This dish is actually more of a bayaldi than a ratatouille, as the ingredients are thinly sliced; in a traditional ratatouille, they are cubed. The difference comes through in the presentation — I layer the vegetables in a ring for visual effect. And the flavors more than deliver on expectations.

SERVES 4

¼ cup/50 ml olive oil

1 onion, diced

2 vine-ripened tomatoes, washed, seeded, and cut into chunks

1 bouquet garni (see p. 10)

1 tbsp/15 ml tomato paste

1 tbsp/15 ml honey

1 clove garlic, germ removed, chopped

salt and pepper

2 zucchini, sliced ⅛ inch (3 mm) thick (optional: peel in strips with a channel knife)

4 Roma tomatoes, sliced ⅛ inch (3 mm) thick

2 Japanese eggplant, sliced ⅛ inch (3 mm) thick

8 piquillo peppers, cut in half, then wedges

3 tbsp/45 ml breadcrumbs

2 tbsp/30 ml chopped flat-leaf parsley

olive oil, for sautéing

Preheat oven to 350°F (180°C).

In a medium-sized nonstick sauté pan over medium heat, cook onions in the olive oil until translucent. Add the vine-ripened tomatoes, bouquet garni, tomato paste, honey, and half the garlic. Season with salt and pepper. Cook until almost all the water evaporates. With a hand-held blender or in a blender, purée the tomato mixture; set aside.

In the same pan over medium heat, lightly sauté the zucchini, Roma tomatoes, eggplant, peppers, and remaining garlic. Season lightly. Don't overcook — they will finish cooking in the oven. Set aside. Ladle the tomato mixture into 4 individual-serving round, shallow ovenproof dishes or 1 larger, round, shallow dish. Arrange the vegetables, alternating by color, upright to form a fan around the perimeter of the baking dishes.

In a mini processor, blend the breadcrumbs, garlic, and parsley until well mixed; sprinkle over top the ratatouille. Bake for 10 minutes or until heated through.

MOULES AU FENOUIL ET PERNOD

Mussels with Pernod and fennel

Between the fennel and the Pernod, it's clear that this dish is all about balancing the mussels with a distinctive licorice taste. The overall effect is subtle. The flavors harmonize nicely and the mussels seem happy to come out of their shells.

SERVES 4

4 lbs/2 kg mussels

1 fennel bulb, cut into thin, uniform strips

4 shallots, finely diced

black peppercorns, crushed or ground

1 cup/250 ml dry white wine

2 tbsp/30 ml Pernod

2 vine-ripened tomatoes, blanched, peeled, seeded, and diced

2 tbsp/30 ml finely chopped chives

½ cup/125 ml unsalted butter, softened

2 tbsp/30 ml chopped parsley

Wash the mussels, discarding any that are open or have an odor.

In a large, heavy-bottomed pot over medium heat, warm the fennel, shallots, a few crushed peppercorns, the wine, and Pernod. Add the mussels, cover the pot, and increase the heat to high. Cook for 3–4 minutes or until the mussels open.

Add the tomatoes and chives, gently toss, then remove the mussels to individual rimmed soup plates or to a single platter. Add the butter to the sauce; whisk.

Drizzle the sauce over the mussels and serve at once, with warm crusty bread.

CABILLAUD EN PAPILLOTE

Black cod in parchment

This is a dish that combines the practicalities of a cooking method with an accent of presentation. The "oven" created by the parchment paper papillote holds in heat and moisture during baking. At the table, the steam and aromas are released when the parcel is opened. The effect is pure theater.

SERVES 4

4 6-oz/170 g black cod fillets

baby green basil pesto (see p. 28)

1 lemon

olive oil, for brushing

2 large (16x20-inch/40x50 cm) sheets parchment paper

12–16 pieces sun-dried tomatoes, julienned

Preheat oven to 325°F (160°C).

Coat the fish on all sides with the pesto. Cut the lemon into 8 slices, discarding the ends. Fold a sheet of parchment paper in half and cut it so that it will be a heart shape or circle when unfolded. Unfold and brush one side of the paper with olive oil, leaving at least a 2-inch (5 cm) un-oiled border. On half of the parchment, lay a bed of tomatoes, top with a fish fillet and then two slices of lemon.

Fold the other half of the parchment over the fish. Working along the open side, seal the parcel by crimping the two edges of parchment together.

Place the papillote parcels on a baking sheet; bake for 10–15 minutes or until the papillote is browned and puffed (the steam from the cooking fish will puff the parchment paper up into a dome).

To serve, transfer the papillote parcels to serving plates, to be opened at the table.

LOUP DE MER EN CROÛTE DE SEL

Branzino in a salt crust

This flavorful, showy dish is perfect for a dinner party. There is a certain satisfaction as you cut away the salt crust and expose the fish. The aroma bursts out at the same time — creating a guaranteed dramatic moment.

SERVES 4

2 1–1½-lb/500–750 g whole
   Mediterranean sea bass, cleaned

3 lbs/1.5 kg coarse kosher or rock salt

1 ¾ cups/425 ml all-purpose flour

4 egg whites

2 tsp/10 ml olive oil

4 sprigs parsley

2 sprigs rosemary

2 sprigs thyme

2 bay leaves

1 tbsp/15 ml crushed black peppercorns

1 lemon, sliced, ends discarded

Preheat oven to 350°F (180°C).

Bring the fish to room temperature. Trim the fins and check that the body cavities of the fish are clean.

In a large bowl, combine the salt, flour, and egg whites; mix to form a grainy paste. Divide the mixture into quarters.

On a large baking sheet covered with parchment paper, make a "platform" by molding a layer of salt mixture large enough for both fish to rest on. Rub the cavity of each fish with the olive oil; stuff them with the parsley, rosemary, and thyme sprigs, bay leaf, peppercorns, and lemon slices. Place the fish on top of the salt bed. Pack the remaining salt mixture over the fish, enclosing it completely.

Bake for about 30 minutes. Remove from the oven; let stand 5 minutes.

To serve at the dinner table, gently crack the salt crust open to expose the fish. Discard the salt layer. Peel off the skin from the top of the first fish. Carefully lift the top fillet from the bones and transfer it to a serving plate. Lift and discard the bones. Gently lift the second fillet off the skin; transfer it to the plate. Repeat with the second fish.

POULET À LA BIÈRE

Chicken with beer

Some foods are best cooked fast and with panache. This is not one of them. Rather, the slowness of the cooking brings out the flavors. The broth shows the influence of the origins of the dish: from near the Belgian border, where they love their beer.

SERVES 4–6

1 4–5 lb/2–2.5 kg grain-fed chicken

salt and pepper

2 tbsp/30 ml olive oil

4 shallots, chopped

6 tbsp/90 ml gin

2 cups/500 ml blonde beer

½ cup/125 ml crème fraîche

1 bouquet garni (see p. 10)

½ lb/250 g button mushrooms

1 egg yolk

1 tbsp/15 ml finely chopped
  flat-leaf parsley

Cut the chicken into pieces; season with salt and pepper.

In a Dutch oven or cocotte, heat the olive oil over high heat. Starting with skin-side down, sear the chicken until golden brown on all sides. Remove from heat and set aside.

Pour off any excess oil in the pot and return the pot to the heat. Add the shallots and cook gently, uncovered, for 1 minute. Return the chicken to the pot.

Add the gin, deglazing the pot by scraping up any browned bits of chicken and shallot left on the bottom. Stir in the beer, crème fraîche, and bouquet garni. Cover and simmer for 30 minutes. Add the mushrooms and cook, uncovered, for 15 minutes or until the liquid is reduced by half. Remove the chicken and mushrooms and keep warm.

In a small bowl, mix the egg yolk with a small amount of the warm sauce (this will prevent the egg from curdling when it is added to the sauce). Pour the tempered egg into the sauce; keep warm but do not return to a boil.

Arrange the chicken and mushrooms on a serving platter; sprinkle with the parsley. Serve with the sauce on the side.

TATIN AUX TOMATES,
HOMARD, ET RATTES

Tomato tatin with lobster and fingerling potatoes

People often serve lobster because it is so easy to cook, but there is more that you can achieve if you can get past just throwing it into the water to boil. In France, we get our best potatoes from the island of Noirmoutier, just off Brittany. Perfect paired with the local lobster.

For a different presentation (and to show off the tatin) serve separately, steaming the lobster in the shell and drizzling with butter.

Note: Frozen puff pastry sheets are available ready-made in the freezer section of most supermarkets. When buying the lobsters, be sure they are alive, as bacteria forms quickly on dead lobsters. To check, pick up the lobster — the tail should curl.

SERVES 4

4 large vine-ripened
   tomatoes, halved

salt and pepper

4 tbsp/60 ml unsalted butter

2 tbsp/30 ml honey

9 oz/250 g savory tart pastry (see p. 14)
   or 1 sheet store-bought puff pastry

2 shallots

2 cloves garlic, germ
   removed, chopped

12 fingerling potatoes, peeled,
   cooked in lightly salted water,
   sliced into 1/8-inch (3 mm) discs

2 lobsters, cooked, meat removed

1 sprig tarragon, chopped

Preheat oven to 350°F (180°C).

Sprinkle the tomatoes with salt to extract their liquid. Drain and place even amounts into four 6-inch (15 cm) cast-iron pans, cut-side up; season with pepper. Dot 2 tbsp/30 ml of the butter equally on the tomatoes, then spread the honey on top. Bake for 5 minutes.

Cover each with one-quarter of the pastry. Bake for another 5–7 minutes or until golden brown.

In the meantime, in a pan over medium heat, sauté the shallots and the garlic with 1 tbsp/15 ml of the remaining butter. Add the potatoes and ¼ cup/50 ml of cold water; simmer for 2 minutes, stirring gently. Add the lobster and cook for about 1 minute or until warmed through. Stir in the remaining 1 tbsp/15 ml of butter. Sprinkle with chopped tarragon to finish.

To serve the tomato tarts, gently run a knife around the rim to loosen, place a plate on top of the pan, and flip over. Repeat with remaining tarts. Top with the lobster and potatoes, and serve.

COQ AU VIN

Chicken in red wine

Each region of France is known for a particular food that best reflects its local offerings. In Burgundy, it is predictably about the wine! For this dish you can either go authentically French, with a red Burgundy, or authentically local, with a comparable Pinot Noir vintage — or try both, since you're likely to make this recipe more than once! Just keep in mind the rule we French follow: good wine makes better food.

Note: The chicken requires marinating for at least 12 hours, so plan ahead. Demi-glace is readily available in fine food shops or some butcher shops.

SERVES 4–6

1 4–5 lb/2–2.5 kg grain-fed chicken

4 cups/1 liter chicken stock
   (see p. 10) or use store-bought

2 tbsp/30 ml olive oil

salt and pepper

2 carrots, chopped

1 onion, chopped

1 shallot, chopped

1 head garlic, unpeeled, halved

1 bouquet garni (see p. 10)

4 cups/1 liter demi-glace

For marinade:

1 head garlic, unpeeled, halved

1 shallot, chopped

1 onion, chopped

2 carrots, chopped

5 black peppercorns

6 cups/1.5 liters dry red wine

1 bouquet garni (see p. 10)

4 tbsp/60 ml Marc de Bourgogne or Cognac

For garnish:

3 ½ oz/100 g pork belly (slab bacon)

½ lb/250 g button mushrooms

½ lb/250 g pearl onions (use frozen
   if fresh are not available), peeled

1 tsp/5 ml sugar

½ tsp/2 ml unsalted butter

1 tbsp/15 ml finely chopped flat-leaf parsley

few sprigs thyme, for garnish

Rinse the chicken and pat dry with paper towel. Cut into 8 pieces and place in a non-metallic dish. In a small bowl, combine the marinade ingredients. Pour over the chicken, cover with plastic wrap, and let marinate, in the refrigerator, for at least 12 hours. Strain, reserving the marinade.

Preheat the oven to 350°F (180°C).

In a small saucepan, bring the chicken stock to a boil, skimming off any impurities that rise to the top.

In the meantime, in a Dutch oven or cocotte, heat the olive oil over high heat. Season the chicken pieces with salt and pepper. Starting with skin-side down, sear the chicken until golden brown on all sides. Drain any excess fat from the pot. Add the carrots, onion, shallots, and garlic; cook for 1 minute. Add the bouquet garni, chicken stock, demi-glace, and the reserved marinade liquid. Bring to a boil, skimming off any impurities that rise to the top. Cover and bake in the oven for 2 hours.

Transfer the chicken to a platter and keep warm. Strain the liquid, return the sauce to the pot, and, on the stovetop over medium heat, reduce the liquid by half. In the meantime, prepare the garnish. Cut the bacon into approximately 1-inch (2.5 cm) strips to make lardons, with a layer of both meat and fat in each. In a skillet over medium heat, sauté the lardons until golden brown. Stir in the mushrooms and cook until a golden brown and tender, about 3 minutes. Drain and set aside.

In a small saucepan or skillet, sprinkle the pearl onions with the sugar. Add the butter and enough water to barely cover the onions. Bring to a boil and simmer, occasionally swirling the onions around to coat evenly, until the onions are cooked through and almost all of the liquid has evaporated — a glaze will develop as the water evaporates, leaving behind a sugar coating. Remove the pan from the heat.

Pour the hot sauce over top the chicken. Spoon the bacon, mushrooms, and pearl onions over the chicken, and sprinkle with the parsley. Garnish with the sprigs of thyme.

ESCALOPE DE VEAU AU COMTÉ

Breaded veal cutlets with Comté cheese

This is the French version of veal scaloppini. The difference? Being French, it is the cheese.

Note: You'll find veal jus in butcher shops and specialty food stores.

SERVES 4

2 tbsp/30 ml dried whole
   morel mushrooms

1 ⅓ lbs/600 g boneless veal strip loin

3 ½ oz/100 g Comté cheese (or 4 slices)

⅓ cup/75 ml all-purpose flour

2 large eggs

1 tbsp/15 ml finely chopped flat-leaf parsley

½ cup/125 ml breadcrumbs

1 cup/250 ml veal *jus*

1 cup/250 ml whipping cream

¾ cup/175 ml unsalted butter

salt and pepper

In a small bowl, pour about 2 tbsp/30 ml boiling water over the morels and let stand to rehydrate.

Trim the strip loin and cut into eight ¼-inch- (5 mm) thick slices. With a mallet, pound each slice to flatten; trim to equal sizes.

Sandwich one slice of Comté cheese between two slices of veal.

Prepare a breading station: assemble a bowl holding the flour, a bowl holding the eggs lightly whisked with the parsley, and a bowl holding the breadcrumbs. Bread the veal by dredging in the flour, dipping in the egg, and finally coating with the breadcrumbs, shaking off any excess. Place the breaded veal on a tray; refrigerate until needed.

Strain the morels, reserving the liquid.

In a saucepan over medium heat, cook the veal jus and morels for 2 minutes. Pour in the cream and mushroom liquid. Simmer slowly until the sauce lightly coats a spoon. In the meantime, melt the butter in a large nonstick sauté pan over medium heat. Cook the veal in the butter, turning once, until golden brown and medium-rare.

Serve with the sauce on the side.

POULET DE GRAIN RÔTI

Roast chicken

Sometimes French cooking is about complexity, and sometimes it is about simplicity. In France, we have a long history with chicken and we have many, many ways to serve it. This dish is the most basic — and it is simply beautiful.

SERVES 4

2 4-lb/2 kg roasting chickens

½ cup/125 ml unsalted butter, softened

salt and pepper

1 head garlic, unpeeled, halved

2 bay leaves

2 sprigs thyme

1 lemon, sliced, ends discarded

½ cup/125 ml composed
  lemon butter (see p. 20)

4 carrots, halved

1 stalk celery, halved

2 onions, halved

Preheat oven to 325°F (160°C).

Rinse the chickens inside and out; pat dry with paper towel. Butter the outside of the chickens and season the cavities with the unsalted butter and salt and pepper. Stuff with the garlic, bay leaves, thyme, and lemon slices. Loosen the skin under the breasts and legs and rub the meat with the composed lemon butter, being careful not to tear the skin. Truss each chicken by placing the bird breast-side up and looping the mid-point of a piece of butcher's twine about 3 times the length of the bird under the tail end then around the ends of the legs. Tie over top of the legs to secure. Run string along either the side of the bird toward the wings, pulling the legs tight against the body. Turn the bird over and bring the string around over the wings. Tie the two ends of the string securely; trim off excess string.

In the bottom of a wide shallow roasting pan, make a bed of carrots, celery, and onions for the chickens to rest on. Lay the birds on top of the vegetables and bake for about 1 hour, turning the birds a quarter turn every 15 minutes, until golden brown. Remove from the oven; let rest for 5 minutes.

To prepare the jus, remove any excess fat from the roasting pan. Place on the stove-top over medium-high heat. Deglaze by pouring in about ½ cup/125 ml cold water and lifting up the bits of food in the bottom of the pan with a wooden spoon. Reduce the heat to medium-low and cook until the sauce has reduced to desired consistency. Strain; keep warm.

Remove strings from chickens. With a sharp knife, cut each chicken in two down the backbone. Serve half a chicken per person, with a drizzle of *jus* and your choice of vegetables.

MAGRET DE CANARD
À L'ORANGE ET GRAND MARNIER

Duck breast with orange and Grand Marnier

This dish is delicious with baby carrots braised with orange and saffron, and with potatoes cooked in duck fat. Duck stock can be found in specialty food shops, butcher shops, and some grocery stores.

SERVES 4

½ tbsp/7 ml each ground coriander, cardamom, ginger, and allspice

3 tbsp/45 ml honey

2 magret duck breasts

2 tbsp/30 ml white vinegar

4 oranges, peeled and segmented

½ tsp/2 ml saffron

3 tbsp/45 ml Grand Marnier

2 tbsp/30 ml Marsala

2 ¼ cups/550 ml duck stock

salt and pepper

In a small bowl, mix the spices with 1 tbsp/15 ml of the honey.

Score the duck, then sear, skin-side down, in a heavy pan over medium-high heat, until crispy. Carefully pour off the rendered fat. Flip the duck and brush with the honey mixture. Cook for another 2 minutes. Remove the duck from the pan and keep warm.

In the same pan, combine the vinegar, remaining honey, orange segments, and saffron; bring to a boil. Stir in the Grand Marnier and Marsala. Pour in the duck stock; season with salt and pepper. Slowly reduce the liquid to desired consistency.

With a sharp knife, slice the duck and transfer to the plate or serving platter; serve at once, with the sauce.

CÔTES LEVÉES DE BOEUF
BOURGUIGNON

Beef short ribs bourguignon

This classic French dish is guaranteed to satisfy every time. It can be prepared in advance; in fact, I think it tastes better when it has had a chance to sit. In my version, I prefer to use a higher quality of meat than most recipes typically call for. To me the concept of quality holds true in every situation. Here my choice of meat is short ribs. *Note: Demi-glace can be found in specialty food shops, butcher shops, and some grocery stores.*

SERVES 6

2 lbs/1 kg beef short ribs, off the bone, cut into approx. 1 ½-inch (4 cm) cubes

salt and pepper

⅔ cup/150 ml all-purpose flour

1 onion, chopped

1 carrot, chopped

½ cup/125 ml chopped celery root

½ leek, white and light green part only, chopped

2 cloves garlic, germ removed, chopped

2 sprigs thyme

1 bay leaf

6 cups/1.5 liters demi-glace

3 cups/750 ml dry red wine

1 bunch young carrots, tops on

16 pearl onions, peeled

¼ lb/125 g pork belly (slab bacon)

4 tbsp/60 ml olive oil

¼ lb/125 g white button mushrooms, quartered

1 tbsp/15 ml finely chopped flat-leaf parsley

Season, then dredge the short ribs in the flour; shake off any excess.

Heat the olive oil in a Dutch oven or large cocotte over medium-high heat. Sear the meat on all sides until golden brown, working in batches if necessary to avoid crowding in the pot. Once all the meat has been seared, drain off any excess fat, and return the pot with the meat to the heat. Add the onion, carrot, and celery root. Sweat the vegetables until soft and translucent; do not allow them to color. Add the leek and garlic; sauté lightly. Add the thyme and bay leaf.

In a heavy-bottomed saucepan, heat the demi-glace and red wine until hot. Remove the short ribs and vegetables from the pot and deglaze the pot with ¼ cup/50 ml cold water, lifting up the brown bits of meat from the bottom of the pot with a wooden spoon, and reducing the liquid by half. Return the beef and vegetables to the pot; add the hot demi-glace–wine mixture. Simmer gently for 1½–2 hours or until the meat is tender.

In the meantime, peel the young carrots, leaving a bit of the green tops on for decoration.

In a small pot of boiling water, cook the pearl onions until tender; set aside. Cook the young carrots the same way; set aside.

Cut the bacon into approximately 1-inch (2.5 cm) strips to make lardons, with a layer of both meat and fat in each. Heat the olive oil in a large sauté pan over medium-high heat. Add the bacon and cook until most of the fat has been rendered. Add the mushrooms; sauté until the bacon is golden and the mushrooms are cooked. Drain on paper towel.

Remove the short ribs from the cooking liquid; set aside, covered, to keep warm. Strain the remaining liquid into a clean saucepan. Over medium heat, reduce the liquid to a sauce consistency, until it coats the back of a wooden spoon evenly. Stir in the mushrooms and onions.

To serve, place some of the beef in a large shallow bowl. Spoon the mushroom–onion sauce on top, garnish with the young carrots, and sprinkle with the parsley.

POULET DE CORNOUAILLES
EN CRAPAUDINE

Quick-roasted Cornish hen

This "crapaudine" gets its French name from the appearance of the bird when prepared for cooking: frog-like. It is flattened to reduce the cooking time and to increase the amount of crispy skin, as more of it is exposed directly to the heat. *Note: This recipe requires marinating the hens for at least 3 hours, or overnight, so plan ahead.*

SERVES 4

2 12-oz/360 g Cornish hens

½ cup/125 ml olive oil

zest of 2 lemons

juice of 2 lemons

2 cloves garlic, germ removed,
   finely chopped

1 sprig thyme, leaves finely chopped

2 tbsp/30 ml composed lemon
   butter (see p. 20), softened

Rinse the hens inside and out; pat dry with paper towel. With poultry shears or a sharp knife, remove the backbones. Split the hens open. Flatten hens and pull out the breastbones — this will help keep the hens flat for even cooking.

In a large non-metallic bowl, combine the olive oil, lemon zest, lemon juice, garlic, and thyme. Coat the hens in the marinade; wrap, and refrigerate for at least 3 hours, or overnight.

Preheat oven to 325°F (160°C).

On a grill or in a hot cast iron fry pan, sear the hens, skin-side down, for 2 minutes. Transfer to a roasting pan and coat with composed lemon butter. Bake for 15 minutes. Remove from the oven; let rest for 5 minutes before serving.

HACHIS PARMENTIER

Shepherd's pie

I never understand why people laugh when I say that this dish can be made with leftover beef bourguignon, but I'm serious. When people think of shepherd's pie, they tend to think of the British-pub version, but the presentation and experience can be much more elevated. Think of this dish as a hearty stew, with a serious change in tone and look.

Note: Form individual portions in ring molds, available in various shapes and sizes in most culinary shops. Choose deep molds that are about the same size as the diameter of the mushrooms.

SERVES 4

4 portobello mushrooms, stems
   and gills removed

2 tbsp/30 ml olive oil

salt and pepper

1 tbsp/15 ml truffle
   paste (optional)

½ cup plus 2 tbsp/150 ml
   unsalted butter

2 shallots, chopped

1 onion, chopped

4 cups/1 liter mashed potatoes
   (leftover is fine)

2 tbsp/30 ml Devon cream
   or 45% cream

1 ¼ lbs/625 g roast beef (leftover),
   ground or shredded

breadcrumbs, for sprinkling

Preheat oven to 375°F (190°C).

Slice the mushrooms (leave the caps whole if forming the pie into individual ring molds). In a skillet over medium heat, sauté the mushrooms in the olive oil. Season with salt and pepper. Add truffle paste, if using. To the same pan, add ½ cup/125 ml of the butter. Sauté the shallots and onions until soft; do not allow to color.

In a bowl, combine the mashed potatoes and cream.

Spread a portion of the mushroom–onion mixture in the bottom of an ovenproof baking dish or casserole dish. Spread a layer of the beef and then another layer of the mushroom–onion mixture, alternating until all has been used. Top with the potatoes. Sprinkle the breadcrumbs over top, and dot with the remaining butter. Bake for 20–30 minutes or until heated through and the top is golden.

To make individual portions, sit the molds on a parchment paper-lined baking sheet. Make a base with the mushroom caps. Press each layer of the mushroom–onion and beef mixtures, and the potatoes, down firmly. Sprinkle with the breadcrumbs; dot with the remaining butter. Leaving the molds in place; bake as directed for single casserole.

CARRÉ DE VEAU
AUX CHANTERELLES ET RAGOÛT DE SALSIFIS
Veal stew with chanterelles and salsify ragout

Salsify is a root vegetable described as having the taste of oysters, with a touch of sweetness. Braised with some type of meat *jus*, it goes well with meats and poultry.

SERVES 4

2 tbsp/30 ml olive oil

½ rack of veal

1 ½ cups/375 ml dry white wine

2 ¼ cups/550 ml white veal stock

1 bouquet garni (see p. 10)

1 sprig thyme

salt and pepper

1 ½ cups/375 ml small
    white mushrooms

2 ¼ cups/550 ml whipping cream

1 ½ cups/375 ml chanterelles, blanched

1 ¼ cups/300 ml unsalted butter

3–4 salsify roots, peeled and
    cut into 2-inch (5 cm) pieces

Heat the oil in a Dutch oven or other heavy-bottomed pot over medium-high heat. Sear each side of the veal in the oil; set aside, discarding the fat left in the pot. To the pot, add the wine, stock, bouquet garni, thyme, and salt and pepper to taste; bring to a boil. Add the white mushrooms and veal, cover, and cook for about 30 minutes.

Remove the meat from the pot and keep warm. Reduce the liquid to half. Add the whipping cream and again reduce the liquid to half. Stir in the blanched chanterelles.

In a pan, melt the butter. Sear the salsify for about 1 minute. Add water to cover, about ½ cup/125 ml; cook the salsify until the liquid evaporates.

Serve the veal with the salsify and mushroom sauce.

POT-AU-FEU

Beef stew

This is a classically French dish in its simplicity and its flavors. The clear broth accents the ingredients without blanketing them, as sometimes happens with a heavier sauce.

Accompany with baby gherkins, Dijon mustard, and grilled or toasted French bread.

SERVES 6

10 cups/2.5 liters cold water
1 lb/500 g beef short ribs
1 lb/500 g beef cheeks, cut into chunks
1 lb/500 g inside round, cut into chunks
1 onion
1 bay leaf
1 clove
1 bouquet garni (see p. 10)
1 head garlic, unpeeled, halved
salt and pepper

6 2-inch (5 cm) beef marrow
   bones, wrapped in cheesecloth
6 carrots, peeled
6 small white turnips, peeled, halved
3 parsnips, peeled
3 leeks, white part only,
   roughly chopped
½ celery root, chopped
1 tbsp/15 ml chopped flat-leaf parsley

In a Dutch oven or cocotte, cover the short ribs, beef cheeks, and inside round with cold water. Bring to a boil and simmer for 1 hour, skimming off any impurities that rise to the top. Clouté the onion by piercing the bay leaf and then the onion with the clove. Add the onion clouté, bouquet garni, garlic, and salt and pepper to taste to the pot; stir; simmer for 1 hour.

Add the marrow bones wrapped in cheesecloth to the pot. Add the carrots, turnips, parsnips, leeks, and celery root. Simmer for 20–30 minutes or until the vegetables are tender.

Remove the meat and bones, discarding the cheesecloth. Arrange with the vegetables on a warm platter. Sprinkle with parsley.

Strain the sauce and serve along with the meat and vegetables.

JARRET D'AGNEAU BRAISÉ AUX ÉPICES

Moroccan-style braised lamb shanks

This Moroccan-style lamb stew reflects France's colonial past. It is fragrant and spicy but not excessively hot. The effect is exotic but not overpowering.

SERVES 4

3 tbsp/45 ml olive oil

4 lamb shanks

1 onion, chopped

1 cup/250 ml dry white wine

1 cup/250 ml chicken stock (see p. 10)
  or use store-bought

1 carrot

1 leek

½ celery root

1 vine-ripened tomato, seeded
  and chopped

1 orange, sliced, end pieces discarded

4 star anise

2 cinnamon sticks

1 bay leaf

1 sprig mint

1 sprig basil

½ head garlic

1 ½-inch (4 cm) piece gingerroot, peeled

1-inch (2.5 cm) piece galangal root, peeled

1 tsp/5 ml coriander seeds

½ tsp/2 ml cardamom

Preheat oven to 325°F (160°C).

Heat 2 tbsp/30 ml of the oil in a Dutch oven. Add the lamb and sear over medium-high heat until well browned. Set aside. Discard the oil, leaving the brown pan drippings — the *sucs* — behind.

In the same pot, sauté the onion in the remaining 1 tbsp/15 ml olive oil. Pour in the wine and stock; deglaze by scraping up the bits of lamb and onion in the bottom of the skillet.

Add the lamb and the rest of the ingredients; bring to a boil. Cover and cook in the oven for about 1½ hours or until the meat is tender. Transfer the lamb and vegetables to a serving platter and keep warm.

Strain the cooking liquid and return to the pot. On the stovetop over high heat, reduce the liquid to the desired consistency for a sauce. To serve, pour the sauce over the lamb shanks.

Desserts
Desserts

GÂTEAU D'ORANGES AU RHUM

Orange cake with rum and citrus candy

This cake holds its moisture very well, making it a perfect dessert for picnic lunches.

Candied citrus is an attractive garnish for cakes, tarts, fruit, ice cream, and sorbets. It can be made from the rind of any citrus fruit. Because citrus pith is bitter, remove as much of it as possible before candying the zest.

Note: Vanilla sugar is easily made at home: put a vanilla bean and sugar into a jar and let it sit for at least a week — though a month is better — to flavor the sugar. Or you can buy it in grocery stores or specialty food shops.

SERVES 6–8

For citrus candy:

2 large oranges

2 tbsp/30 ml sugar

For cake:

²/₃ cup/150 ml sugar	¹/₃ cup/75 ml unsalted butter, melted
2 tbsp/30 ml vanilla sugar	3 tbsp/45 ml rum (white or dark)
4 egg yolks	4 egg whites
²/₃ cup/150 ml all-purpose flour	pinch of salt

To make the citrus candy: with a knife or vegetable peeler, cut the zest off the oranges as closely as possible to the surface, leaving as much of the white pith behind as possible. Cut the zest into very thin strips. Blanch for 2 minutes in boiling water; strain. Repeat blanching process 3 times, to eliminate bitterness.

In a small pot, heat the sugar with 2 tbsp/30 ml water. Add the blanched zest and simmer gently for 5–10 minutes or until the zest is soft and slightly transparent. Remove the zest with a slotted spoon and cool on a rack. Stored in an airtight container, the citrus candy will keep for several months.

To make the cake, preheat oven to 400°F (200°C).

Chop the candied orange zest. Whisk the sugar, vanilla sugar, and egg yolks together. Gradually add the flour. Add the melted butter, 1 tbsp/15 ml of the rum, and the candied orange zest.

In a metal bowl, whip the egg whites along with a pinch of salt until soft peaks form. Gently fold into the batter with a spatula.

Pour the batter into a loaf pan. Bake for 10 minutes, then reduce heat to 350°F (180°C). Bake for about 20 minutes or until the top is golden and a toothpick inserted in the center comes out clean.

Remove the cake from the oven. While it is still hot, drizzle the remaining 2 tbsp/30 ml of rum over top. Cool in the pan on a wire rack for 10 minutes, then turn the cake out to finish cooling.

Serve with vanilla ice cream, crème anglaise, or an orange salad.

ÎLES FLOTTANTES

Floating islands

This classic French dessert falls well within the category of comfort foods. My version is light, as it calls for no cream — and therefore perfect after a heavy meal.
Note: This dessert can be prepared 6–12 hours in advance. Store refrigerated, covered carefully with plastic wrap (the plastic will stick to the surface, so don't allow it to touch).

SERVES 4

butter and flour to coat pan

6 egg whites

pinch of salt

½ cup/125 ml sugar

juice of 1 lemon

Preheat the oven to 325°F (160°C).

Butter and lightly dust with flour a baking ring mold that is approximately 8 inches (20 cm) in diameter and 2 inches (5 cm) deep, or a square cake pan of similar dimensions.

In a bowl, whisk together the egg whites with a pinch of salt. Whisk for at least 5 minutes, until firm peaks form. Continue whisking, gradually adding the sugar. Slowly add the lemon juice, whisking constantly. Pour the batter into the pan and bake for 5–10 minutes or until the top is a very pale golden color. Remove from the oven; let cool in the mold. Once cool, cut into square or round shapes with a cookie cutter. Refrigerate until ready to serve.

Serve with crème anglaise and a drizzle of hot caramel.

SOUFFLÉ AU GRAND MARNIER

Grand Marnier soufflé

There's an old expression that you wait for a soufflé, it doesn't wait for you. With a soufflé, timing is everything: it must be served as soon as it is ready. At a dinner party, the host will be forgiven for disappearing into the kitchen for 20 minutes once this light treat makes its appearance.

Note: The pastry cream can be made up to 2 days in advance; store in the refrigerator.

SERVES 4

For pastry cream:

2 cups/500 ml whole milk	4 egg yolks
ice, for ice bath	⅓ cup/75 ml cornstarch
⅔ cup/150 ml sugar	4 tbsp/60 ml Grand Marnier

For soufflé:

butter and sugar, to coat soufflé dish	juice of ½ lemon
4 egg whites	6-cup/1.5 liter soufflé dish or
pinch of salt	individual ramekins
¼ cup/50 ml sugar	powdered sugar, for dusting

To make the pastry cream, bring the milk to a boil in a heavy-bottomed pot. As soon as it starts to boil, set aside to cool slightly. In the meantime, fill a large bowl with ice, to be used later for cooling.

In a bowl small enough to fit inside the bowl of ice, whisk together the sugar and egg yolks until the mixture is thick but light. Add the cornstarch, stirring to mix well. Slowly strain in the hot milk, a little at a time, whisking gently until incorporated.

Transfer the mixture to the pot, returning the now-empty bowl on top of the ice. Bring the mixture to a boil, whisking constantly. If lumps form, remove the pot from the heat and whisk the mixture until smooth, then return it to the heat. As soon as the mixture reaches the boil, pour it into the bowl sitting on the ice. As it cools, gently stir the mixture occasionally. Once it is cooled completely, cover the bowl with plastic wrap and refrigerate. Just before use, whisk the mixture until light. Add the Grand Marnier, whisking until incorporated.

To make the soufflé, preheat oven to 400°F (200°C).

Butter a soufflé dish well; dust with sugar.

In a medium-large bowl, whisk the egg whites with a pinch of salt until stiff peaks form. Slowly add the sugar and beat until glossy, making a meringue. Add the lemon juice, a little at a time, stirring to incorporate.

With a spatula, fold one-quarter of the egg whites into the prepared pastry cream. Gently fold that mixture into the remainder of the meringue. Pour into the prepared dish, filling to the top. Tap the dish hard on the countertop several times to get rid of any air bubbles.

Flatten and smooth the surface with a pallet knife or spatula. Use a clean, dry cloth to wipe off any excess egg mixture from the rim, then gently run the point of a knife around the edge of the dish to break the surface tension and allow the soufflé to rise more easily.

Bake for 10 minutes. Reduce the heat to 350°C (180°C); cook for another 5 minutes or until the soufflé is puffed and light brown. Do not open the oven door during the baking time. Remove from heat, dust with powdered sugar, and serve at once.

GÂTEAU AUX BANANES

Banana cake

The fruitiness and rum in this favorite come directly from the French islands. This fresh-tasting and flavorful dessert will be appreciated at dinner, lunch, or any occasion.

SERVES 6–8

½ cup/125 ml unsalted butter, melted

⅔ cup/150 ml sugar

2 eggs

1 cup/250 ml all-purpose flour

1 ½ tsp/7 ml baking powder

⅔ cup/150 ml ripe mashed banana

½ cup/125 ml cream cheese, softened

Preheat oven to 350°F (180°C).

In a medium-sized bowl, cream the butter and sugar together. Stir in the eggs. Add the flour and baking powder, stirring to mix. Stir in the banana and cream cheese. Pour the batter into a lightly greased and floured loaf pan. Bake for 25–35 minutes or until a toothpick inserted into the center comes out clean.

Serve with rum anglaise or rum-flavored ice cream.

TARTE AU CITRON

Lemon tart

As I often say, good food comes down to choices of complexity and simplicity. Do you balance flavors or present them in their purest form? In this dish, the intention is to bring forward the pure power of the lemon flavor. It is intense, and it is wonderful.

MAKES ONE 9-INCH (23 CM) TART

9 oz/250 g sweet tart pastry (see p. 15)

4 eggs

1 ¼ cups/300 ml powdered sugar

½ cup/125 ml unsalted butter, melted

zest of 3–4 lemons

juice of 4 lemons

Blind bake the tart shell (see p. 14). Set to one side on a rack to cool slightly.

Reduce the oven temperature to 300°F (150°C).

In a medium bowl, whisk together the eggs and sugar. Add the melted butter, lemon zest, and lemon juice, stirring to mix well. Pour the batter into the still slightly warm tart shell; bake for about 15 minutes or until the filling has set. Remove from heat and let cool.

Serve with vanilla ice cream.

TARTE TARTIN

Upside-down caramelized apple tart

This is a perfect winter dessert. The tart is cooked upside down and retains the shape of the pan when served — it looks simply wonderful. Serve it with vanilla ice cream or crème fraîche.

Note: Frozen puff pastry sheets are available ready-made in the freezer section of most supermarkets.

SERVES 4

¼ cup/50 ml unsalted butter
2–3 tbsp/30–45 ml powdered sugar
butter and sugar, for topping

4 Granny Smith apples, peeled, cored, and cut into large wedges, reserving any off-cuts
9 oz/250 g savory tart pastry (see p. 14) or 1 sheet store-bought puff pastry

In an 8-inch (20 cm) ovenproof skillet or baking pan over medium heat, melt the butter. Sprinkle the sugar evenly over top.

Place the apple wedges in the skillet, fitting the pieces tightly together in a concentric circle on top of the sugar, filling the skillet completely. Slice any apple off-cuts and pile them on top; dot with butter and a pinch of sugar.

Gently cook the apples over low heat for 15–20 minutes or until the sugar has caramelized to a medium-brown color. Don't rush this step; as the apples soften and cook, they produce juice, which must evaporate before the caramel will form. During cooking, gently press the apples down and make sure they're filling the bottom of the pan. When cooked, remove the skillet from the heat but do not remove the apple tart.

In the meantime, preheat the oven to 400°F (200°C), or the recommended temperature for the pastry if store-bought. Roll out the pastry to a circle just slightly larger than the size of the skillet or baking pan. Score the pastry to make air vents. Working quickly, set the pastry on top of the tart, covering it completely. Trim off any excess pastry. Bake for 20–25 minutes or until the pastry is a golden brown. Remove from the oven; let the tart cool in the pan for 10 minutes. Gently reheat the tart on the stovetop for a few minutes to loosen it in the skillet. Turn out upside down onto a serving plate. The tart will not be completely set and the caramel will be runny. Serve warm.

MOUSSE AU CHOCOLAT
ET AUX FRUITS SECS

Chocolate mousse with dried fruits

Always a favorite with children, a flavorful mousse is the perfect way to end a meal. It is rich and sweet but not too heavy. And not all French cuisine is for fancy entertaining … in France, we keep this in the refrigerator as an energy snack or a casual sweet.

Note: As the mousse needs to be refrigerated for at least 6 hours, this is an ideal dessert to make a day in advance.

SERVES 4

1 tbsp/15 ml finely diced dried apricots

1 tbsp/15 ml finely diced dried cranberry

1 tbsp/15 ml finely diced dried mango

2 tbsp/30 ml Grand Marnier

1 ½ cups/375 ml dark chocolate chips

½ cup/125 ml cold unsalted butter, diced

¼ cup/50 ml whipping cream

5 eggs, separated

pinch of salt

Marinate the dried fruit in Grand Marnier for 1 hour.

Melt the chocolate chips in the top of a double boiler or in a bowl over a pot of simmering water.

Slowly add the butter to the melted chocolate, stirring until incorporated. Stir in the cream.

In a large bowl, beat the egg yolks slightly, then pour in the warm chocolate mixture, a little at a time so as to not scramble the eggs, until incorporated. Stir in the marinated fruits.

Whip the egg whites with a pinch of salt until firm peaks form; fold into the chocolate mixture. Spoon the mousse into parfait glasses and refrigerate for at least 6 hours.

To serve, top with whipped cream, finely diced fruit sprinkles, or chocolate shavings, and dust with powdered sugar.

SORBET À LA CRÈME SUR

Sour cream sorbet

This tangy treat offers a nice counterpoint to sweet dishes. Serve it with a chocolate tart, orange cake, or another sweet treat.

SERVES 4

½ cup/125 ml sugar

3 ½ cups/875 ml sour cream

1 ⅓ cups/325 ml yogurt

juice of 1 lemon

juice of 1 orange

To make the simple syrup, dissolve the sugar in ½ cup/125 ml water in a pot over low heat, stirring occasionally until the mixture is clear. Increase the heat to bring the mixture to a boil. Remove from heat and let cool.

In a stainless steel bowl, whisk the simple syrup, sour cream, yogurt, and lemon and orange juices together until smooth. Pour into an ice-cream maker. Make the ice cream according to manufacturer's directions.

CRÈME GLACÉE À LA VANILLE

Vanilla ice cream

Most people don't realize that vanilla offers a broad range of flavors, depending in part on where it is grown. French cuisine's relationship with the bean comes from France's colonial past.

By making your own ice cream, you ensure that nothing but the freshest ingredients are used, with no preservatives. You will also discover something you may not have known about plain old vanilla.

Note: Vanilla sugar is easily made at home: put a vanilla bean and sugar into a jar and let it sit for at least a week — though a month is better — to flavor the sugar. Or you can buy it in grocery stores or specialty food shops.

MAKES ABOUT 4 CUPS/1 LITER

3 cups/750 ml whole milk

1 Tahitian vanilla pod

3 espresso (dark roast) coffee beans

8 egg yolks

¾ cup/175 ml sugar

2 tbsp/30 ml vanilla sugar

1 cup/250 ml whipping cream

In a heavy-bottomed pot, warm the milk. Add the vanilla pod and coffee beans and bring the milk to a boil. As soon as the milk starts to boil, remove the pot from the heat; let steep for 10 minutes. Strain, discarding the coffee beans but reserving the vanilla pod.

In a bowl, whisk the egg yolks, sugar, and vanilla sugar until the mixture is thickened, about 3–4 minutes. Gently stir in the hot milk, a small amount at a time. Return the custard mixture to the pot and heat gently, stirring constantly until the custard thickens. Do not allow to boil, or the custard will curdle. The custard is ready when you can draw your finger across the back of a custard-coated spoon and the trail stays clean. Remove from heat. Stir in the cream.

Cut the vanilla pod lengthwise and scrape the vanilla seeds into the custard. Transfer the custard to an ice-cream maker. Make the ice cream according to manufacturer's directions.

CRÈME CARAMEL

Caramel custard

Some dishes make more of an impression than their preparation deserves. Crème caramel is actually very hard to get wrong. Just don't overcook it. Otherwise, keep it simple and enjoy the flavors and the accolades.

SERVES 4

1 ¾ cups/425 ml sugar

4 cups/1 liter whole milk

6 eggs

½ vanilla bean or 1 ½ tsp/7 ml
 pure vanilla extract

To make the caramel, in a small, heavy-bottomed saucepan, just cover ³⁄₄ cup/175 ml sugar with water. Cook until the water evaporates and the sugar caramelizes to a rich amber shade. Remove from the heat and let any bubbles subside. Evenly cover the bottom of 4 individual ramekins or a 4-cup/1 liter soufflé dish with the caramel.

Preheat the oven to 325°F (160°C).

To make the custard, bring the milk, along with the vanilla bean or vanilla extract, to a boil in the top of a double boiler or in a bowl over a pot of simmering water. Remove from the heat and let stand to infuse, 10–15 minutes.

In a large bowl, mix the eggs with the remaining 1 cup/250 ml of sugar, incorporating well.

Remove the vanilla bean from the milk, and reserve. Slowly add the infused milk to the egg and sugar mixture, stirring until fully incorporated. Strain the custard through a fine-mesh strainer.

Cut the vanilla bean lengthwise and scrape out the seeds. Stir the seeds into the custard.

Pour the custard into the ramekins or soufflé dish. Set into an ovenproof pan; fill the pan with enough hot water to reach halfway up the side of the ramekins or dish. Bake for 25–30 minutes or until just set and a skewer inserted in the center comes out clean. Chill the baked custard completely before serving. To unmold, run the tip of a sharp knife around the inside edge of each ramekin. Invert onto a deep dish or wide plate. The caramel will run out over top.

SABAYON DE FRAISES GRATINÉES

Strawberries gratin with sabayon

In this elegant dessert, the fresh strawberries are perfectly accented with the sabayon —
a very light, foamy custard.

SERVES 4

½ cup/125 ml fresh strawberries,
    stems on

4 tbsp/60 ml Cointreau

4 tbsp/60 ml Riesling

¼ cup/50 ml sugar

2 egg yolks

1 egg

1 sprig mint, finely chopped

Wash the strawberries, leaving the stems and any leaves on. Air dry; remove the stems
and leaves, and halve (quarter, if using large berries).

    Combine the Cointreau and Riesling in a small bowl. Add the berries and let sit
for 10–15 minutes. Strain and set aside, reserving the liquid.

    In a medium-sized metal bowl, whisk together the sugar, egg yolks, and whole
egg. Whisk in the reserved Cointreau–Riesling mixture. Place the bowl over a pot of
simmering water, or transfer the mixture to a double boiler, and gently cook while
whisking to add air to the mixture. The sabayon is done when it becomes shiny and
forms a ribbon when the whisk is lifted up.

    Spoon the strawberries into an ovenproof serving dish, cover with the sabayon, and
put under the broiler until golden. Garnish with a sprinkle of chopped mint and serve
at once.

CLAFOUTIS AUX FRAMBOISES

Raspberry clafoutis

Traditionally, this dish is made with cherries. The raspberries in this recipe are a nice substitute and a real flavor surprise, especially because the two fruits look so similar in the cake. The effect is a dessert-based trompe l'oeille that works very nicely.

SERVES 4

9 oz/250 g sweet tart pastry (see p. 15)

2 cups/500 ml fresh
   raspberries, unwashed

¾ cup/175 ml sugar

4 eggs

1 cup/250 ml Devon cream or 45% cream

2 ½ tbsp/40 ml Chambord

Blind bake the tart shell (see p. 14).

   Arrange the raspberries in the bottom of the tart shell.

   In a bowl, whisk together the sugar and eggs. Whisk in the cream and Chambord. Pour the mixture into the tart shell over the raspberries and bake in a 350°F (180°C) oven for 20–30 minutes.

Index